HOPE
IN THE SHADOW
OF ARMAGEDDON

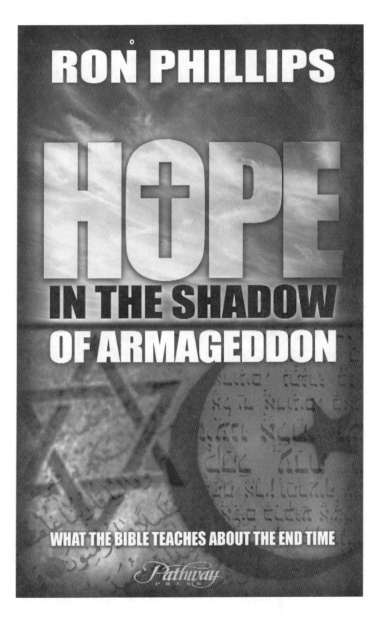

RON PHILLIPS

H+PE

IN THE SHADOW
OF ARMAGEDDON

WHAT THE BIBLE TEACHES ABOUT THE END TIME

Pathway
PRESS

Unless otherwise indicated, Scriptures are from the *New King James Version.* Copyright © 1979, 1980, 1982, 1990, 1995, Thomas Nelson Inc., Publishers.

Scripture quotations marked KJV are taken from the King James Version of the Bible.

Scripture quotations marked *NIV* are taken from the *Holy Bible, New International Version®.* Copyright © 1973, 1978, 1984 by International Bible Society. Used by permission of Zondervan Publishing House. All rights reserved.

Scripture quotations marked *NASB* are taken from the New American Standard Bible®. *NASB.* Copyright © The Lockman Foundation 1960, 1962, 1963, 1968, 1971, 1972, 1973, 1975, 1977. Used by permission.

Scripture quotations marked *NLT* are taken from the Holy Bible, *New Living Translation,* copyright © 1996. Used by permission of Tyndale House Publishers, Inc., Wheaton, Illinois 60189. All rights reserved.

Scripture quotations marked *TM* are from *The Message.* Copyright © 1993. Used by permission of NavPress Publishing Group.

Book Editor: Wanda Griffith
Editorial Assistant: Tammy Hatfield
Copy Editors: Elizabeth Hightower
Cresta Shawver

Library of Congress Catalog Card Number: 2003116370
ISBN: 0-87148-148-8
Copyright © 2004 by Pathway Press
Cleveland, Tennessee 37311
All Rights Reserved
Printed in the United States of America

Dedication

When I think of the word *hope*, several friends come to mind. These are friends who have lifted up my spirit and given me hope time and again.

To these four couples, all members of Central, I dedicate this book:

Frank and Martha Steil
Matt and Beverly Hammon
Ken and Elizabeth Higgins
Jeff and Sheri Carmichael

Also, I dedicate this book to a dear friend of this ministry, Mr. David Parker, president and CEO of Covenant Transport, who is a constant encouragement to me.

Contents

Acknowledgments

I want to express my deepest gratitude and thanks to . . .

Paulette, my wife, who gives me hope every day!

Doug Wright for his Spirit-inspired artistry that graces the front cover.

Carolyn Sutton and *Karen Newberry* for typing and transcribing.

Margy Barber, whose editorial skills and support make this writing ministry possible.

Angie McGregor, who pushed this project to completion.

The members of Central who have supported my preaching for nearly 25 years. You are a joy!

Introduction

As I gathered my thoughts in preparing for this book, I browsed through my personal library and found an old volume titled *Signs of the Time*, by the late M.R. DeHaan. The book was first released in 1951. Remarkably, the book is still accurate and relevant. The reason it has lasted is that Dr. DeHaan stuck with the Scripture, not speculation.

While these may be the most exciting and fearful days we have ever experienced, we must not rest upon speculation and emotion, but we must stand upon the teachings of the Word of God, rightly divided. It is too easy to speculate about the evil brought about by world leaders.

Before the capture of Saddam Hussein, some people believed he was the Antichrist and that Babylon would literally be rebuilt. He was even referred to at times as Nebuchadnezzar reincarnated. The truth is, he was a dictator, hidden behind the cloak of religion, who will one day die and stand before God.

Over the years it has been speculated in turn that Hitler, Mussolini, the Shah of Iran, the king of Spain, Kissinger, Gorbachev, or a host of others were Antichrist. It is embarrassing when over time such teaching has proven to be false, and even worse, the witness of Christ has been hindered. Many reacted fearfully in the mid 1980s when some prophet supposedly predicted the date of Jesus' coming. The predicted date came and went, and we still await Christ's coming. The powerful truth of the second coming of Christ suffered a blow from the false teachers' predictions.

So, I have set pen to paper to write a book in these last days—a book filled with hope rather than fear and speculation. I intend to let the Bible speak about end times. I fully believe that the Rapture is real and precedes the judgments of the Tribulation and the millennial reign of Christ on the earth. However, I do believe that the church must be returned to Pentecostal power before these events can occur. Scripture says in Acts 3:19-21:

> Repent therefore and be converted, that your sins may be blotted out, so that times of refreshing may come from the presence of the Lord, and that He may send Jesus Christ, who was preached to you before, whom heaven must receive until the times of restoration of all things, which God has spoken by the mouth of all His holy prophets since the world began.

Jesus will not rapture the church until it is restored. The church has become complacent and spotted with disunity and division. She must turn her heart to the

Bridegroom, for Christ is not coming for a hag or a whore, but He is coming for a glorious bride!

Paul wrote to the church at Thessalonica about the end times. Many in his day were fearful that they had missed the Rapture. Even though Paul focused on the theme of judgment, he was encouraging the church constantly. Jesus delivers us from judgment. First Thessalonians 1:10 says, "Wait for His Son from heaven, whom He raised from the dead, even Jesus who delivers us from the wrath to come."

Paul gave hope and joy about the return of Jesus: "For what is our hope, or joy, or crown of rejoicing? Is it not even you in the presence of our Lord Jesus Christ at His coming?" (2:19).

Paul exhorted the body to live holy lives in anticipation of His coming "so that He may establish your hearts blameless in holiness before our God and Father at the coming of our Lord Jesus Christ with all His saints" (3:13).

Also, we are to receive comfort as we await the coming of the Lord.

> For the Lord Himself will descend from heaven with a shout, with the voice of an archangel, and with the trumpet of God. And the dead in Christ will rise first. Then we who are alive and remain shall be caught up together with them in the clouds to meet the Lord in the air.

And thus we shall always be with the Lord. Therefore comfort one another with these words (4:16-18).

The church does not have an appointment with the wrath of God. Jesus is not coming to abuse His bride!

For God did not appoint us to wrath, but to obtain salvation through our Lord Jesus Christ, who died for us, that whether we wake or sleep, we should live together with Him. Therefore comfort each other and edify one another, just as you also are doing (5:9-11).

Our lives can be lived in peace of heart as we await His coming.

Now may the God of peace Himself sanctify you completely; and may your whole spirit, soul, and body be preserved blameless at the coming of our Lord Jesus Christ. He who calls you is faithful, who also will do it (5:23, 24).

Finally, even the rise of the Antichrist, the son of perdition, is no cause for alarm.

Now, brethren, concerning the coming of our Lord Jesus Christ and our gathering together to Him, we ask you, not to be soon shaken in mind or troubled, either by spirit or by word or by letter, as if from us, as though the day of Christ had come. Let no one deceive you by any means; for that Day will not come unless the falling away comes first, and the man of sin is revealed, the son of perdition (2 Thessalonians 2:1-3).

You see, we are not to be shaken and disturbed, but we are to live in hope. The grace of God that saved us will see us through.

> For the grace of God that brings salvation has appeared to all men, teaching us that, denying ungodliness and worldly lusts, we should live soberly, righteously, and godly in the present age, looking for the blessed hope and glorious appearing of our great God and Savior Jesus Christ (Titus 2:11-13).

There are indeed fearful times coming in the Tribulation period: the Antichrist, world tyranny, shortages, famines, disasters and the final battle of Armageddon. We are called to live in hope and not fear. I trust this book will give you *Hope in the Shadow of Armageddon.*

At the time of this writing, Saddam Hussein has been captured and mighty shifts are happening in the Middle East.

The ancient hatreds continue to boil to the surface in Israel as well as in Afghanistan, Iraq and Iran. When will all of this end? You will see this is not a national or international conflict—it is the first war without national boundaries. This war rages on earth with countless innocent casualties. Blood flows in the streets of Jerusalem, Jericho, Istanbul, Baghdad and Riyadh. Clearly, this war is also being waged on a higher level. It is a conflict of immense spiritual proportions. The infernal forces of "the lie" parade their insidious terror under the flag of religion! Yet, truth will triumph! All of these things cause us to look up and to look ahead to "the blessed hope." My prayer is that the truth in this book will replace fear with faith and terror with triumph!

We're being shown how to turn our backs on a godless, indulgent life and how to take on a God-filled, God-honoring life. This new life is starting right now, and is whetting our appetites for the glorious day when our great God and Savior, Jesus Christ, appears (Titus 2:12, 13, *TM*).

1
Countdown to Armageddon

E very time I turn on the radio or TV or pick up a newspaper, I am reminded that war wages in the Middle East once again. Our nation and its allies are working together, trying to bring peace. The eyes of the world are focused on the Middle East. Afghanistan, Iraq, Israel and the Palestinian territories are ablaze with terror.

The Bible predicted a future filled with great trouble and war at the end. The campaign of all campaigns predicted by Scripture is to take place at Armageddon. Many believe we are at the beginning stages of that last war.

Jesus made predictions about the last days in all of the Gospels. There is one nation at the focal point of the end-time events—the nation of Israel. In prophecy, we often see the nation of Israel referred to as "the fig tree." At the end of the age, Israel must be an independent nation with Jerusalem under her control.

As we turn our eyes eastward and watch the events of war unfold, I believe we can see the shadow of Armageddon beginning to fall. While it is true that "no one knows the day or the hour" when end-time prophecies will be fulfilled or when the Lord Jesus will return (Matthew 24:36, *NLT*), we can still recognize the times and the seasons.

Our Lord Jesus left us clear teachings concerning His second coming. Let us hear His servant Paul speak to us of the clear signs that the end is near.

> But concerning the times and the seasons, brethren, you have no need that I should write to you. For you yourselves know perfectly that the day of the Lord so comes as a thief in the night. For when they say, "Peace and safety!" then sudden destruction comes upon them, as labor pains upon a pregnant woman. And they shall not escape. But you, brethren, are not in darkness, so that this Day should overtake you as a thief" (1 Thessalonians 5:1-4).

Jesus rebuked the Pharisees because they were able "to discern the appearance of sky, but . . . not . . . the signs of the times" (Matthew 16:3, *NASB*). As Christians, we should watch for the signs Jesus gave us in Matthew 24, Mark 13, Luke 21, and 2 Timothy 3:1-5. In all of these passages, I find that only one sign has been fulfilled in our generation: the return of the Jewish nation to their national homeland!

The Shadows Over Israel

Israel recently celebrated 50 years as a nation in our modern world. It was May 1948 when the United Nations partitioned what was then called *Palestine* and declared a portion of the land to be named *Israel*. A nation was reborn in a day!

Israel became the only nation to die and be reborn in world history! Three times the nation has been exiled and then returned to its homeland:

- When famine swept the land in the time of Jacob, the nation went to Egypt to survive under the watchful and wise care of Joseph. Over the course of time, they found themselves enslaved in Egypt, but Moses led them with a mighty hand to their Promised Land.

- Under the rule of King Nebuchadnezzar, they were taken into captivity in Babylon, but they rebuilt their land.

- In A.D. 70, Israel was conquered by Rome. The Roman hordes swept into Jerusalem and sacked the land. A few years later, Rome even changed the name of Jerusalem to Aelia Capitolina and forbade Jews to come within a furlong of the city. Israel appeared to be dead. But in 1948, the dried bones of a dead Israel came together, and the nation lives!

There are four signs of the end times I call *shadows* that loom in our society and throughout the world.

1. *The Shadow of Natural Disaster.* There will be "signs in the sun, in the moon, and in the stars . . . the sea and the waves roaring" (Luke 21:25). In the last 20 years, we have been plagued with an increase in natural disasters—hurricanes, floods, volcanoes, winter storms that cripple whole regions, droughts and famine on almost every continent. Members of the mass media have focused heavily on such themes for movies and documentaries.

It seems the whole earth has literally been shaking and convulsing for the past three decades. Romans 8:22 declares that, indeed, "creation groans and labors." This groaning is the death rattle of the old order of sin. This travail will lead into the birth of a new world order: that of Jesus Christ! The earth shook at the death of Jesus, and it will surely shake again at the time of His coming!

2. *The Shadow of Human Desperation.* The rise of mental health issues in our world is alarming. Stress seems to be growing on every level, including . . .

- Personal stress, as we cope with the individual disasters that fall upon us.

- Family stress and fractures, with about half of marriages ending in divorce and a generation of children living in houses that aren't really homes.

- Business and financial uncertainty building, with market collapses and economic turmoil. The rate of heart attacks and suicides often rises concurrently with increasing financial stress.

- National and international stress, enhanced by the apparent lack of moral character that many societies, including our own, have fallen into. Corruption, terrorism and violence abound in many countries in our generation, such as Somalia, Bosnia, Russia, Northern Ireland, Afghanistan, Iraq and most areas of the Middle East.

3. *The Shadow of Preoccupation.* The sign of Noah was "preoccupation." Everybody in Noah's day was doing their own thing; no one really cared about the warnings of that crazy man who was building a boat! There was an immense indifference leading to the moral decline of the world in Noah's day. Character no longer mattered. It was a day when evil reigned.

And as it was in the days of Noah, so it will be also in the days of the Son of Man: They ate, they drank, they married wives, they were given in marriage, until the day that Noah entered the ark, and the flood came and destroyed them all (Luke 17:26, 27).

The parallels to our day are clear. Our society is too busy to care! God must help us and deliver us from an insane preoccupation with the trivial and unimportant. We need revival as never before here in America!

4. *The Shadow of Perversion.* In the days of Sodom and Gomorrah, marriage fell by the wayside. The homosexual agenda had taken over the city. Lot was a leader in Sodom, but as the lone godly voice in a city of evil, he could not stand against the power of the homosexual lobby.

"Likewise as it was also in the days of Lot: They ate, they drank, they bought, they sold, they planted, they built; but on the day that Lot went out of Sodom it rained fire and brimstone from heaven and destroyed them all. Even so will it be in the day when the Son of Man is revealed. In that day, he who is on the housetop, and his goods are in the house, let him not come down to take them away. And likewise the one who is in the field, let him not turn back. Remember Lot's wife. Whoever seeks to save his life will lose it, and whoever loses his life will preserve it. I tell you, in that night there will be two men in one bed: the one will be taken and the other will be left. Two women will be grinding together: the one will be taken and the other left. Two men will be in the field: the one

22

will be taken and the other left." And they answered and said to Him, "Where, Lord?" So He said to them, "Wherever the body is, there the eagles will be gathered together" (Luke 17:28-37).

These Old Testament judgments cry out to us to repent! Jesus is coming! Our generation must heed the warnings. It seems today's society loves everything in life more than God, and fears anything but God! Second Timothy 3:1-5 gives the prophecy:

But know this, that in the last days perilous times will come: For men will be lovers of themselves, lovers of money, boasters, proud, blasphemers, disobedient to parents, unthankful, unholy, unloving, unforgiving, slanderers, without self- control, brutal, despisers of good, traitors, headstrong, haughty, lovers of pleasure rather than lovers of God, having a form of godliness but denying its power. And from such people turn away!

Reading these scriptures, it is clear that the shadow of Armageddon is falling. But I believe there is hope! Jesus said, "When these things begin to come to pass, then look up, and lift up your heads; for your redemption draweth nigh" (Luke 21:28, KJV). We must remember, this verse tells Christians that our hope is just around the corner, but to the lost it says, "Your doom draws near!"

The late Reverend W.A. Luckie once told me this story. A little girl and her dad were swimming and the tide started to go out, catching the little girl on her float in its ebb. The dad knew if he tried to swim out to her in an attempt to bring her to shore, they might both drown, because the tide was pulling her out to sea. So he shouted, "Honey, float on your air mattress—I will come for you as quickly as I can!" He ran for help, but despite his haste, it took four hours for him and a rescue boat to locate the air mattress floating out in the sea. They were amazed to find the little girl floating calmly and smiling. She said, "I knew you would come, Daddy! You said you would!"

As the flood of darkness fills this world, I'm glad that my Savior has promised that He is coming! The old hymn written by Winfield Macomber says it well:

> Oft methinks I hear His footsteps,
> Stealing down the paths of time;
> And the future dark with shadows,
> Brightens with this hope sublime.
> Sound the soul-inspiring anthem;
> Angel hosts, your harps attune;
> Earth's long night is almost over,
> Christ is coming—coming soon.
> Earth's long night is almost over,
> Christ is coming—coming soon.
>
> —Winfield Macomber, 1890

2
Ancient Weapons and Modern Terror

R ecent incidents have inflamed the conflict in the Middle East to the breaking point. After years of talking peace, all the peace efforts now seem to be lost. Both sides are pointing fingers at each other.

Do not keep silent, O God! Do not hold Your peace, and do not be still, O God! For behold, Your enemies make a tumult; and those who hate You have lifted up their head. They have taken crafty counsel against Your people, and consulted together against Your sheltered ones. They have said, "Come, and let us cut them off from being a nation, that the name of Israel may be remembered no more." For they have consulted together with one consent; they form a confederacy against You: The tents of Edom and the Ishmaelites; Moab and the Hagrites; Gebal, Ammon,

and Amalek; Philistia with the inhabitants of Tyre;
Assyria also has joined with them; they have helped
the children of Lot. Selah (Psalm 83:1-8).

The news media portray a distorted picture of what
is going on in the Middle East. As a result, much of
the public is ill-informed about the issues surrounding
events worldwide. But what does God say about this
conflict? Where and when did these hostilities begin?

The Scripture clearly gives us a history of this conflict, shows us the long-lasting results of sin, and
reveals truth about the Middle East and the second
coming of Christ. Most of all, the Bible gives us hope
in fearful times.

Would you believe that all of the strife between
Middle Eastern nations began 3,000 years ago when a
man slept with a woman who was not his wife, and
their union resulted in the birth of a child?

Origins

It is important to understand the birth of the conflict
in the Middle East. We must journey back in time to
the tents of Abraham. God had called Abraham from
the city of Ur of the Chaldeans to follow Him into the
land we now call Israel. Along the way, God promised
Abraham a son by Sarah, his wife. During a season of
famine, Abraham went down to Egypt, where he nearly lost his wife and his life through compromise!

Among the things he brought back from Egypt was a handmaiden for his wife, Sarah. The girl's name was Hagar.

Egypt gives us such a strong picture of the world and its influence. Sooner or later, every worldly thing you try to latch onto will cost you.

God had promised Abraham and Sarah that they would bear a son who would be blessed. As the years went by and they grew old together, the days of child-bearing passed for Sarah. Doubting God's word of promise to them and His timing, they decided to take matters into their own hands. Sarah convinced her husband to take her handmaiden Hagar as a concubine or surrogate mother. So Abraham conceived his first son, Ishmael, by this servant girl.

Ishmael's descendents are the Arabs and Palestinians of today. One of Abraham's grandsons, Esau, married one of Ishmael's daughters, and their union developed into the Arab race.

Even though Ishmael was not the promised child God had planned for Sarah and Abraham, God didn't turn His back on him. In grace and mercy, God promised, "As for Ishmael, I have heard you. Behold, I have blessed him, and will make him fruitful, and will multiply him exceedingly. He shall beget twelve princes, and I will make him a great nation" (Genesis 17:20).

The great Arab nation and its abundant wealth give

witness to the promise of God, even to this day! In spite of this abundance, Ishmael's heritage was to be unsettled and warlike. "He shall be a wild man; his hand shall be against every man, and every man's hand against him. And he shall dwell in the presence of all his brethren" (16:12).

Note the characteristics of Ishmael's people:

- Wild

- Aggressive

- Hostile

- Warlike

- Stubborn and uncompromising

- Living east of Israel.

As we read in Genesis, Abraham and Sarah eventually, and miraculously, conceived a child of their own. From this union came Isaac—the child God had promised them. Isaac would have a son of his own named *Jacob*, whom God would later rename *Israel*. Division between the two brothers, Ishmael and Isaac, was inevitable and has continued throughout the years. Ishmael's descendants have always been determined to annihilate Israel.

The hatred between the two factions still rages on. In October of 2000, Palestinian Television broadcasted excerpts from an Islamic sermon preached in the

Zayed bin Sultan Aal Nahyan mosque in Gaza. The Middle East Media Research Institute supplied a translation that was emailed to me:

> The Jews are Jews, whether Labor or Likud. . . . They do not have any moderates or any advocates of peace. They are all liars . . . O brother believers, the criminals, the terrorists are the Jews, who have butchered our children, orphaned them, widowed our women and desecrated our holy places and sacred sites. They are the terrorists. They are the ones who must be butchered and killed, as Allah the Almighty said, "Fight them."

Contemporary History

Israel had known great blessing and expansion under David and Solomon. But subsequent years brought on idolatry and immorality, and God drove them into exile. Now in our lifetime, we have seen the rebirth of the nation Israel.

As briefly stated earlier, Israel was completely plundered and ravaged many times in ancient history. I have put together a basic timeline of the major conflicts, based on the historical and public record:

- The first conflict was in Egypt, when Pharaoh Amenhotep I tried to eliminate the nation by killing all the firstborn of Israel. God stepped in, destroying Egypt's army in the Red Sea and delivering His people.

- Israel was plundered again in 722 B.C. by Assyria, under the leadership of Sargon II. His son, Sennacherib, later depopulated much of Israel in cold blood. This evil ruler died by the hand of an assassin.

- The Temple in Jerusalem was destroyed and more Jews were violently carried captive to Babylon in 586 B.C. They survived the over-throw of that Empire! Under the rule of Cyrus, they were allowed to return home.

- Around 473 B.C., Persia conquered and occu-pied Israel. King Xerxes' evil counselor, Haman, tried to persuade him to annihilate the Jews. God sent a young woman named Esther, who became queen in 478 B.C. and saved the nation. Haman died on the gallows he had built for the purpose of murdering Jews.

- In 169 B.C., the insane Antiochus Epiphanes of Syria captured Jerusalem. He offered a pig (considered unclean by the Jews) on the sacred altar and put Israel to the sword. Yet he died, and the nation lived on.

- In A.D. 70, Rome came against Israel. That final overthrow was accomplished by the ruler Titus, and Jerusalem was destroyed as predicted by Jesus in Luke 21:

But when you see Jerusalem surrounded by armies, then know that its desolation is near. Then let those who are in Judea flee to the mountains, let those who are in the midst of her depart, and let not those who are in the country enter her. For these are the days of vengeance, that all things which are written may be fulfilled. But woe to those who are pregnant and to those who are nursing babies in those days! For there will be great distress in the land and wrath upon this people. And they will fall by the edge of the sword, and be led away captive into all nations. And Jerusalem will be trampled by Gentiles until the times of the Gentiles are fulfilled (vv. 20-24).

• From 1939 to 1945, an evil cloud in Germany arose against the Jewish nation. Evil men were alarmed at the thought of the Jews regrouping into a nation. The waters had been stirring for some time. In 1894, Theodore Herzl, a Hungarian Jew, called for a centralized location for the Jewish nation. He was spurred on by the persecution in France of Alfred Dreyfus, a Jewish military officer. His fervent stand stirred interest about a Jewish homeland. Later, Chaim Weizmann, a Jew living in Britain who had rendered exceptional service to Britain during the war, asked for a special reward in honor of his service; he wanted help in establishing a homeland for the Jews in Palestine. This led Lord Balfour, head of Britain's foreign office, to issue a declaration, pledging to bring this about.

- In 1917, General Allenby liberated Palestine from the Ottomans, and in 1922, the League of Nations conferred a mandate on Great Britain to establish a national home for the Jews. A sizeable homeland, called the Emirate of Transjordan, was established in an agreement as a homeland for Arabs in the area. This became the country of Jordan, ruled by the Hussein family of Saudi Arabia.

- Just before Germany began the horrible campaign against Jews, Britain made a concession to the Palestinian Arab population and betrayed the Jewish people. Britain issued the infamous White Paper of 1939, severly limiting the number of Jews who could emigrate from Europe to Israel. As a result, many Jews who would have fled Europe were not able to, and millions faced Hitler's gas chambers and ovens. Hitler's obsession with creating a perfect race and finding a "final solution" to eradicate the Jews would lead to the death of 6 million Jews.

(See Hal Lindsey's book, *The Everlasting Hatred*, for even more background about this ancient conflict between Arabs and Jews.)

Israel Reborn

A conscience-stricken world gave Israel back its land on November 29, 1947, when the United Nations partitioned what was called Palestine. Palestine was not then, nor has it ever been, a true nation. The Turks simply ruled over what was called "Palestine" as a part of the Ottoman Empire.

The British once again moved forward with promises of a homeland for the Jews. Saudi Arabia immediately stood against these intentions, its leaders boldly predicting the eventual annihilation of Israel by the Arab world. Arabs everywhere once again picked up the mantle of Jewish hatred.

On May 14, 1948, Israel declared itself a state, and the Arabs declared war. However, the Arabs were defeated, in spite of the fact that they outnumbered Israel 100 to 1!

Wars have erupted in modern times—in 1956, 1967, 1973—even in our current day. Yet, Israel lives on, a nation touched by the eternal hand of God.

Heaven's View of the Middle East

The Palestinian people were supposed to have

Jordan, yet they were thrown out by Lebanon. The land of Gaza is rightly theirs, yet their hatred of Israel makes it impossible for them to make a deal and find peace. Yasser Arafat, president of the Palestinian Council, was offered all the territory prior to the 1967 War, but he refused it. The purpose of the militant Arab world has not changed: their goal is the destruction of Israel.

God made it clear in Scripture that Israel would be returned to its homeland. Palestine has a right to exist as a nation as long as the people stay in harmony with God's plan for the nation of Israel.

The last war of the end times will be fought over these lands. Jesus will come for His people before this final war occurs. How should Christians respond?

1. We must be careful to share the truth and shun liberal propaganda. Be discerning as you listen to news and reports.

2. Understand the times by studying Scripture and being informed.

3. Watch and be ready for the coming of Christ! The time is coming!

4. Promote and support Israel, because Israel is still the apple of God's eye.

3
Jerusalem: A Stone in the World's Shoe

J erusalem may well be the capital city of the universe! According to *Strong's Exhaustive Concordance,* the city is mentioned 881 times in Scripture—667 times in the Old Testament and 144 in the New Testament. No city on earth has seen more and experienced more than this ancient city. Today, it is again the focus of world attention.

The burden of the word of the Lord against Israel. Thus says the Lord, who stretches out the heavens, lays the foundation of the earth, and forms the spirit of man within him: "Behold, I will make Jerusalem a cup of drunkenness to all the surrounding peoples, when they lay siege against Judah and Jerusalem. And it shall happen in that day that I will make Jerusalem a very heavy stone for all peoples; all who would heave it away will surely be cut in pieces, though all nations of the earth are gathered against it" (Zechariah 12:1-3).

I still can recall the emotions that swept over my soul the last time I stood in the ancient city of Jerusalem. During the 14 trips I've made to the Middle East, I've visited Israel, Egypt, Jordan and Lebanon. I never tire of going to Jerusalem and walking through the streets where Jesus once walked.

When you enter the part of Jerusalem called the "Old City," you will find some of the same types of vendors that sold their wares in Jesus' day. They still have the spices and the foodstuffs out in open stalls. When you walk through the Old City, you will likely take the path of the *Via Dolorosa*, or "the way of the cross."

Along with the old, you can look around from that place and see tall, modern buildings as well. You see a city that has swept out of those ancient walls and is now reaching out into the hills of Judea. You look at it and wonder, *Could anything be more beautiful on the face of the earth, especially considering what God did here?*

The Mystery of Jerusalem

The first mention of Jerusalem in Scripture is in Genesis 14:18, where the city is called *Salem*, the city of Melchizedek. Melchizedek, a king-priest, ruled the city. He has been thought by scholars to stand as a type of Christ, a picture of the Messiah who was to come.

> For this Melchizedek, king of Salem, priest of the Most High God, who met Abraham returning from the slaughter of the kings and blessed him, to whom also Abraham gave a tenth part of all, first being translated "king of righteousness," and then also king of Salem, meaning "king of peace" (Hebrews 7:1, 2).

Later in history, Salem came to be called Jebus, the stronghold of the Jebusites. God commanded David to conquer that city. First Chronicles 11:4 records, "And David and all Israel went to Jerusalem, which is Jebus, where the Jebusites were, the inhabitants of the land." Thereafter, David called the name of the city *Jerusalem*, which means "foundation of peace."

God chose the city for His own! His claim is eternal, and is necessary for the outworking of His plan. God made clear statements about this special city.

- "My city" (Isaiah 45:13)

- "My holy mountain" (Isaiah 11:9)

- "The holy city" (Nehemiah 11:1)

God clearly loves this city! Psalm 87:1, 2 says, "His foundation is in the holy mountains. The Lord loves the gates of Zion more than all the dwellings of Jacob."

The Majesty of the City

Jerusalem was given many beautiful names in the Bible:

- City of God—"There is a river whose streams shall make glad the city of God, the holy place of the tabernacle of the Most High" (Psalm 46:4).

- City of Joy—"Why is the city of praise not deserted, the city of My joy?" (Jeremiah 49:25).

- City of Righteousness—"I will restore your judges as at the first, and your counselors as at the beginning. Afterward you shall be called the city of righteousness, the faithful city" (Isaiah 1:26).

- City of the Great King—"Beautiful in elevation, the joy of the whole earth, is Mount Zion on the sides of the north, the city of the great King" (Psalm 48:2).

Those are just a few of the glorious descriptive names of Jerusalem. This city was where David first established worship and where Solomon built the Temple. Jerusalem is where Jesus died on the cross and arose from the grave. And Jerusalem is where Jesus will return!

The Misery of the City

Jerusalem has experienced siege, war and misery. The city has been destroyed and rebuilt many times. Ezra and Nehemiah and later, Herod, had the job of rebuilding the city at different times in its history. After the Romans destroyed the city, Hadrian changed Jerusalem's name again, to the new name of *Aelia Capitolina*. During the crusades, the Muslim nation called it *Al-Quds* or *The Holy*. Muslims still refer to Jerusalem by that name.

Although Jerusalem stands restored today, she is still divided. On the western end of the Temple mount stands the Dome of the Rock—the third holiest site of Islam. Just beyond that building is the Al-aqsa Mosque, towering above the ancient Western Wall of Solomon's Temple, which is known as the Wailing Wall.

While some of the holiest places of Islam are located in Jerusalem, Christianity's greatest treasures are there as well. Bethlehem, the city where Christ was born, is a suburb of Jerusalem. The Temple Mount is the place where Jesus astonished the great teachers when He was only 12 years old. The Via Dolorosa, the way of the cross, is a cherished landmark. Golgotha, the place of the skull and the site of the Crucifixion, is located in the city. The Garden Tomb and the Mount of Olives are among the special places where Jesus walked, talked and taught within the great city of Jerusalem.

Jerusalem holds a legacy of war. The great armies of the world have marched across the land: Pharaoh and Egypt, Assyria and Babylon, Alexander the Great of Greece, the powerful Roman legions, the Ottoman Empire and the armies of Great Britain.

Even in modern history, it holds a record of great conflicts:

- War of Independence—1948
- Six Days' War—1967
- Yom Kippur War—1973
- Intifada—1987
- Today's conflict, from 2000 until the present.

Yes, Jerusalem is a burdensome stone!

"Roadmap for Peace" or Highway to Hell?

According to Michael Evans, in his book *Beyond Iraq*, the so-called "Roadmap for Peace" aims to settle the problems in Israel and the Palestinian territories by the year 2005. This agreement is sponsored by the United States, the European Union, the United Nations and Russia.

Make no mistake: the goal of the militant Muslim is to seize control of East Jerusalem. The final fight and issue behind the conflict between the nations will be Jerusalem as our text predicts.

The Magnificence of That City

Jerusalem will be the last and final city to rule the world! God will cause this earthly city to survive. Our task today is to support the city. Isaiah 40:1, 2 says, "'Comfort, yes, comfort My people!' says your God. 'Speak comfort to Jerusalem, and cry out to her, that her warfare is ended, that her iniquity is pardoned; for she has received from the Lord's hand double for all her sins.'"

Psalm 51:18 reminds us, "Do good in Your good pleasure to Zion; build the walls of Jerusalem."

One day God will establish a New Jerusalem. What a stunning sight it will be when the heavenly city descends! The traveling city, set up in stationary orbit, will drift over earthly Jerusalem!

And he carried me away in the Spirit to a great and high mountain, and showed me the great city, the holy Jerusalem, descending out of heaven from God, having the glory of God. Her light was like a most precious stone, like a jasper stone, clear as crystal. Also she had a great and high wall with twelve gates, and twelve angels at the gates, and names written on them, which are the names of the twelve tribes of the children of Israel (Revelation 21:10-12).

Look also at Hebrews 12:22-24:

But you have come to Mount Zion and to the city of

the living God, the heavenly Jerusalem, to an innu-merable company of angels, to the general assembly and church of the firstborn who are registered in heaven, to God the Judge of all, to the spirits of just men made perfect, to Jesus the Mediator of the new covenant, and to the blood of sprinkling that speaks better things than that of Abel.

Look at the noble population of glory! You and I can be a part of that select number. Gone will be the memories of the hatred and conflict that plague today's world. In that day, the beautiful city of Zion will shine with the brightness of our precious Savior, Jesus Christ!

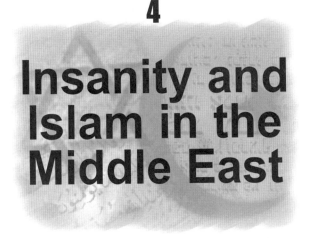

4

Insanity and Islam in the Middle East

E zekiel was a prophet to Israel during their exile to Babylon—a time of judgment on the nation for their idolatry. The final chapters in the Book of Ezekiel describe the future of Israel and the alignment of nations even into our modern day. There we find the pathway to Armageddon clearly laid out.

Prophecy of Israel's Banishment

As we discussed earlier in this book, Israel became a possession of other nations. Then in A.D. 70, Israel was destroyed and its people were scattered across the face of the earth.

Thus says the Lord God: "Because the enemy has said of you, 'Aha! The ancient heights have become our possession,' therefore prophesy, and say, 'Thus says the Lord God: "Because they made you desolate and swallowed you up on every side, so that you became the possession of the rest of the nations, and you are taken up by the lips of talkers and slandered by the people". . . . therefore thus says the Lord God: "Surely I have spoken in My burning jealousy against the rest of the nations and against all Edom, who gave My land to themselves as a possession, with whole-hearted joy and spiteful minds, in order to plunder its open country"'" (Ezekiel 36:2, 3, 5).

Israel also became the plunder of other nations. This little state of Israel has been invaded and possessed by the Romans, the Ottomans, the armies of the Crusades, the British and the Arabs. In Ezekiel 36:4 we read, "Therefore, O mountains of Israel, hear the word of the Lord God! Thus says the Lord God to the mountains, the hills, the rivers, the valleys, the desolate wastes, and the cities that have been forsaken, which became plunder and mockery to the rest of the nations all around."

We've also seen that Israel bore the shame of the nations. I believe the following verse carries a clear word about God's view of the Holocaust. The nations of the world shamefully stood by while the Jewish nation was nearly eliminated.

Therefore prophesy concerning the land of Israel, and

say to the mountains, the hills, the rivers, and the valleys, "Thus says the Lord God: 'Behold, I have spoken in My jealousy and My fury, because you have borne the shame of the nations.' Therefore thus says the Lord God: 'I have raised My hand in an oath that surely the nations that are around you shall bear their own shame' " (vv. 6, 7).

Israel's treatment was the shame of the world. Hitler's terrors in Germany alarmed the world, and at long last, Israel was given her homeland.

Israel's Return

God scattered the nation as a result of their sin. Verse 19 points out, "So I scattered them among the nations, and they were dispersed throughout the countries; I judged them according to their ways and their deeds."

However, God promised that the nation would be regathered. God has never cancelled the covenant of the land. "For I will take you from among the nations, gather you out of all countries, and bring you into your own land. Then I will sprinkle clean water on you, and you shall be clean; I will cleanse you from all your filthiness and from all your idols" (vv. 24, 25).

God promised the nation eventual abundant life and prosperity. Israel has yet to realize this fully. But God always will do what He promises!

I will give you a new heart and put a new spirit within you; I will take the heart of stone out of your flesh and give you a heart of flesh. I will put My Spirit within you and cause you to walk in My statutes, and you will keep My judgments and do them. Then you shall dwell in the land that I gave to your fathers; you shall be My people, and I will be your God. I will deliver you from all your uncleanness. I will call for the grain and multiply it, and bring no famine upon you. And I will multiply the fruit of your trees and the increase of your fields, so that you need never again bear the reproach of famine among the nations. . . . So they will say, "This land that was desolate has become like the garden of Eden; and the wasted, desolate, and ruined cities are now fortified and inhabited" (vv. 26-30, 35).

Prophecy of Israel's Birth

When we turn to Ezekiel 37, the story continues. The valley of dry bones pictures Israel scattered and dead among the nations. The inquiry, "Can these bones live?" (v. 3) raises the fundamental question of Israel's survival. Yet the nation lives today! What has helped this great nation survive?

First of all, Israel lives because of the Word of God. God's Word brings the bones of a dead Israel together. When the Word goes forth, life comes!

The hand of the Lord came upon me and brought me out in the Spirit of the Lord, and set me down in the midst of the valley; and it was full of bones. Then He caused me to pass by them all around, and behold, there were very many in the open valley; and indeed they were very dry. And He said to me, "Son of man, can these bones live?" So I answered, "O Lord God, You know." Again He said to me, "Prophesy to these bones, and say to them, 'O dry bones, hear the word of the Lord'" (vv. 1-4).

Israel has survived because of the Spirit of God. The creative breath of God brings life to God's chosen people. Here is the wind of the Spirit! From the lips of God comes a life-giving breeze that raises up a nation!

Also He said to me, "Prophesy to the breath, prophesy, son of man, and say to the breath, 'Thus says the Lord God: "Come from the four winds, O breath, and breathe on these slain, that they may live."'" So I prophesied as He commanded me, and breath came into them, and they lived, and stood upon their feet, an exceedingly great army. Then He said to me, "Son of man, these bones are the whole house of Israel. They indeed say, 'Our bones are dry, our hope is lost, and we ourselves are cut off!' Therefore prophesy and say to them, 'Thus says the Lord God: "Behold, O My people, I will open your graves and cause you to come up from your graves, and bring you into the land of Israel. Then you shall know that I am the Lord, when I have opened your graves, O My people, and brought you up from your graves. I will put My Spirit in you, and you shall live, and I will place you in your own land. Then you shall know that I, the Lord, have spoken it and performed it," says the Lord'" (vv. 9-14).

Israel has held on as a nation in anticipation of a new King and a new Temple. God will raise up a monarch in Israel, and the Temple will be rebuilt. All of this is surely coming!

> David My servant shall be king over them, and they shall all have one shepherd; they shall also walk in My judgments and observe My statutes, and do them. Then they shall dwell in the land that I have given to Jacob My servant, where your fathers dwelt; and they shall dwell there, they, their children, and their children's children, forever; and My servant David shall be their prince forever. Moreover I will make a covenant of peace with them, and it shall be an everlasting covenant with them; I will establish them and multiply them, and I will set My sanctuary in their midst forevermore. My tabernacle also shall be with them; indeed I will be their God , and they shall be My people. The nations also will know that I, the Lord, sanctify Israel, when My sanctuary is in their midst forevermore (vv. 24-28).

Prophecy of Israel's Battle

After Israel is fully restored and Jerusalem is totally under Jewish control, the Bible says that a great battle will take place. The restored church will have been raptured out of the earth and God will be doing a new, mighty work among the Jewish nation.

> After many days you will be visited. In the latter years you will come into the land of those brought back from the sword and gathered from many people on the mountains of Israel, which had long been desolate; they were brought out of the nations, and now all of them dwell safely (38:8).

The end-times enemy of Israel is named *Rosh*, which is usually interpreted to mean Russia. Ezekiel 38:1-3 addresses those involved in this attack:

> Now the word of the Lord came to me, saying, "Son of man, set your face against Gog, of the land of Magog, the prince of Rosh, Meshech, and Tubal, and prophesy against him, and say, 'Thus says the Lord God: "Behold, I am against you, O Gog, the prince of Rosh, Meshech, and Tubal." ' "

In an alliance with some Arab states, Russia will follow Egypt into Israel. Russia will have some allies in this battle, as told in verses 5 and 6: "Persia, Ethiopia, and Libya are with them, all of them with shield and helmet; Gomer and all its troops; the house of Togarmah from the far north and all its troops—many people are with you."

Persia is modern-day Iran and Iraq. Ethopia and Libya are still in existence today, and they oppose Israel. Gomer's identity is not clear, but some scholars believe it may refer to Europe, and most feel that Togarmah refers to modern-day Turkey. These nations will align with Russia to begin the war of all wars. Read what Scripture says about the arrival of these armies:

> After many days you will be visited. In the latter years you will come into the land of those brought back from the sword and gathered from many people on the mountains of Israel, which had long been desolate; they were brought out of the nations, and now all of them dwell safely. You will ascend, coming like a storm, covering the land like a cloud, you and all your troops and many peoples with you. Thus says the Lord God : "On that day it shall come to pass that thoughts will arise in your mind, and you will make an evil plan: You will say, 'I will go up against a land of unwalled villages; I will go to a peaceful people, who dwell safely, all of them dwelling without walls, and having neither bars nor gates'—to take plunder and to take booty, to stretch out your hand against the waste places that are again inhabited, and against a people gathered from the nations, who have acquired live-stock and goods, who dwell in the midst of the land.

Sheba, Dedan, the merchants of Tarshish, and all their young lions will say to you, 'Have you come to take plunder? Have you gathered your army to take booty, to carry away silver and gold, to take away livestock and goods, to take great plunder?' " (vv. 8- 13).

Here are the allies of Israel. Most believe that Sheba is Egypt, Dedan is Saudi Arabia, the "merchants of Tarshish" references Europe, and the young lions are Britain and America! Could this be America's future? This gives us assurance that America will survive the last days.

God's fury will be poured out in the midst of the battle. Verse 22 says, "And I will bring him to judgment with pestilence and bloodshed; I will rain down on him, on his troops, and on the many peoples who are with him, flooding rain, great hailstones, fire, and brimstone."

The armies opposing Israel will be destroyed. Read Ezekiel 39:1-6:

And you, son of man, prophesy against Gog, and say, "Thus says the Lord God: 'Behold, I am against you, O Gog, prince of Rosh, Meshech, and Tubal; and I will turn you around and lead you on, bringing you up from the far north, and bring you against the mountains of Israel. Then I will knock the bow out of your left hand, and cause the arrows to fall out of your right hand. You shall fall upon the mountains of

Israel, you and all your troops and the peoples who are with you; I will give you to birds of prey of every sort and to the beasts of the field to be devoured. You shall fall on the open field; for I have spoken,' says the Lord God. And I will send fire on Magog and on those who live in security in the coastlands. Then they shall know that I am the Lord."

All of these events will magnify the great name of the Lord! God will receive glory for Himself and bring judgment on the Enemy as seen in 36:23:

And I will sanctify My great name, which has been profaned among the nations, which you have profaned in their midst; and the nations shall know that I am the Lord when I am hallowed in you before their eyes.

The order of events is laid out clearly: Israel, once dead, is again alive and is now victorious. The church will leave through the Rapture before this war. Yet at this moment, the nations are aligning in a last day's scenario.

Knowing the coming events, no one should wait to get his or her house in order! If you need to give your life to Christ, you must not wait!

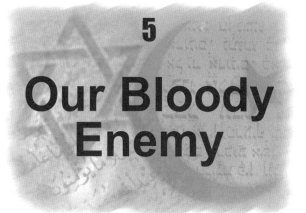

5

Our Bloody Enemy

Islam is a religion of demonic origin and Satanic terror. As you read through historic records, you uncover the fact that the leader of this religion, Mohammed, had a life and a sword stained with the blood of the innocent. Islam's record is a river of blood shed violently in order to obtain more territory.

Only in the last century was the powerful Ottoman Empire finally defeated and the Holy Land freed. The Turks left Israel, but Muslims remained opposed to the resettling of the land by the Jews. Also, the Palestinian Islamic Order supported Hitler and his program of systematic elimination of Jews. Four times the Arab populations declared war on Israel and lost at every turn.

Islamic militants step forward in bold acts of violence in their ongoing battle against those who oppose them. Public record, research and news reports have established that militant Islam was behind many treacherous acts in the past few years. They have . . .

- Sent suicide bombers to kill the innocent
- Murdered Marines in the barracks of Lebanon
- Blown up the U.S.S. *Cole*
- Dragged our soldiers' bodies through the streets of Somalia
- Had Daniel Pearl confess to being a Jew before cutting his throat and broadcasting the video of the event to the world
- Attacked the World Trade Center on September 11, 2001
- Tried to destroy the Pentagon
- Attempted to murder our president on that same day
- Killed our young men and women serving in Iraq and Afghanistan. They hate the Jew, the Christian and the American.

Demonic Islam and Terror

Our battle today stretches beyond the sands of

Iraq, the mountains of Afghanistan and the streets of Jerusalem. This war reaches into the invisible realm Scripture calls *the heavenlies*. While our national leaders fight with weapons of the flesh, we must understand that the battle must be won in the spiritual realm.

Ephesians 6 makes it clear that Satan has ranks of warriors, including principalities, powers and rulers of the dark forces of evil. These ranks are organized to take the planet. They operate in the religious realm.

Satan was the high angel of worship in heaven before his fall. He was anointed as a worshiper to cover the earth with the glory of God. But he turned from God, fell to the earth and took a position, along with one-third of the angels. Satan's goal is to deflect the worship of the Lord Jesus Christ to himself—to rob God of His glory!

Ancient Hatred

The prophet Ezekiel gives us a remarkable outline of end time events in chapters 35—39. As we look at these chapters, they become contemporary and read like the morning paper!

> Moreover the word of the Lord came to me, saying, "Son of man, set your face against Mount Seir and prophesy against it, and say to it, 'Thus says the Lord God: "Behold, O Mount Seir, I am against you; I will

stretch out My hand against you, and make you most desolate; I shall lay your cities waste, and you shall be desolate. Then you shall know that I am the Lord. Because you have had an ancient hatred, and have shed the blood of the children of Israel by the power of the sword at the time of their calamity, when their iniquity came to an end, therefore, as I live," says the Lord God, "I will prepare you for blood, and blood shall pursue you; since you have not hated blood, therefore blood shall pursue you" ' " (35:1-6).

Mount Seir represents the Arab nations that have pursued an ancient hatred of Israel that stretches back to the tents of Abraham.

A Finger in God's Eye—A Bloody Relic

God has an everlasting covenant with Israel whereby it is given the land that is now in dispute. This possession of the land was dependant on their obedience to Yahweh. Periodically, they were dispossessed for a season, but God always brought them back.

Islam demands its adherents' absolute loyalty. Their goal is to rule the whole world through terror and fear. Ultimate loyalty in Islam is the Islamic agenda, even if it means the individual betrays his own nation.

It is time to crack down on the hoodlums hiding

behind the robes of religion. Treason cannot be tolerated in our great, free land! Islam is a religion of anarchy and has at its root a demon god. Its history is bloody and backward, its claims false and its record dastardly. From the subordination and mutilation of women to the cold-blooded murder and terror attacks against innocent lives, Islam has forfeited its right to exist without careful scrutiny from the free world.

Today there is no Islamic country that allows freedom of religion! Furthermore, their hatred of both Jews and Christians is horrific. In Islam, we face more than just a philosophy that crosses all boundaries. Islam is not a choice or simply a belief system—it is a national entity with armies, weapons and wealth, a nation without borders! This ancient religion that claims to be against idols, still worships a black meteorite that was a part of paganism until Mohammed declared it holy.

Islam denies the deity of Jesus Christ and His saving blood, the Holy Trinity, and the Scriptures as we know them. Islam is a religion lost in the past, yet funded by the wealth of its oil fields, it continues its forward march of evil.

Religion and the End Time

In his book, *The Everlasting Hatred*, Hal Lindsey quotes Ayatollah Khomeini, Islamic leader of Iran:

"Islam cannot be defeated. It will be victorious in all the countries of the world." That belief still stands as the ringing cry of many.

Psalm 83:1-8 states:

> Keep not thou silence, O God: hold not thy peace, and be not still, O God. For, lo, thine enemies make a tumult: and they that hate thee have lifted up the head. They have taken crafty counsel against thy people, and consulted against thy hidden ones. They have said, Come, and let us cut them off from being a nation; that the name of Israel may be no more in remembrance. For they have consulted together with one consent: they are confederate against thee: The tabernacles of Edom, and the Ishmaelites; of Moab, and the Hagarenes; Gebal, and Ammon, and Amalek; the Philistines with the inhabitants of Tyre; Assur also is joined with them: they have helped the children of Lot. Selah (KJV).

Islam's Deadliest Deception

Daniel heard the testimony of Michael the archangel, how he fought the principality (a demon of power) in Persia for two weeks. Satan will go to any lengths to receive worship from the blinded people in Islam. Strong spiritual forces are arrayed against the church and against Israel.

Arising out of the Islamic world, the Antichrist will come, speaking peace when there is no peace. As Islam means "peace," so the Antichrist will declare peace. He will consolidate all religions and deny God. He will eventually turn on Islam, and declare that he, rather than even Allah, is the one true God. His false prophet will claim to be Jesus, and together they will plunge the world into seven years of terror. The final battle, as we have read in Ezekiel 38, will reveal Russia and Islamic countries in league together.

Until the End

We must pray that God will break the Islamic strongholds over the people of the world that they may come to Jesus. Let us rest in hope that Jesus will return soon.

6
Is Osama bin Laden the Antichrist?

Ever since he entered the world spotlight, many people have been asking the question, "Is Osama bin Laden the Antichrist mentioned in Scripture?" All over the Middle East, rumors are flying that he is more than an ordinary man.

Those of the Islamic faith are expecting the coming of an end-time Messiah they call the Mahdi. On more than one occasion, certain Imams (holy men) have been declared to be the Mahdi. On January 9, 1980, 63 people across Saudi Arabia were beheaded by the government for their involvement in a raid on the Grand Mosque in Mecca. Why did the raid occur? Because a certain Juhasman claimed to be the end-time leader and his followers were urged to make his cause known. Others who have been rumored to be the Mahdi include the late Ayatollah Khomeini, Yasser Arafat and Saddam Hussein. The truth is that fundamentalist Islam is expecting to see a revelation of the Mahdi in our time!

Followers of Islam believe that when the Mahdi comes, he will be joined by Jesus. Together they are supposed to go to Mecca, where Jesus will deny that He is God, and allow the Mahdi to lead a prayer.

There is now a movement in Islam to declare Osama bin Laden as the Mahdi. He could then summon all Muslims to a jihad, or holy war, to kill the enemies of Allah. It is easy to be fooled by the moderate Muslim speakers, who talk of peace and goodwill. But it is important to remember—their goal is to take over the world.

It is strange indeed how Osama has taken on a Jesus-like appearance. Noted Bible scholar, Perry Stone, makes the following points in his book, *Unleashing the Beast*:

- Bin Laden is from Saudi Arabia; this is where the Mahdi is supposed to originate.

- Bin Laden was willing to wage war with the greatest superpowers in the world.

- Islamic scholars believe that the 21st century will be the century of Islam. Think about a man in a cave in Afghanistan waging war on the nations of the world!

Is Osama bin Laden the Antichrist?

I do not personally believe Osama is the Antichrist. I do believe, however, that he operates with the spirit of an antichrist. I agree with Perry Stone that the Antichrist will arise from the Muslim world. In the end, the Antichrist will be revealed as a phony Muslim, denying the basic confession of Islam that there is no God but Allah. The Antichrist will rise in the Middle East, but he will rise above all religions to declare himself the ultimate deity and god of the earth.

Revelation 13:1-3 tells us what to expect in the coming of the Antichrist.

> Then I stood on the sand of the sea. And I saw a beast rising up out of the sea, having seven heads and ten horns, and on his horns ten crowns, and on his heads a blasphemous name. Now the beast which I saw was like a leopard, his feet were like the feet of a bear, and his mouth like the mouth of a lion. The dragon gave him his power, his throne, and great authority. And I saw one of his heads as if it had been mortally wounded, and his deadly wound was healed. And all the world marveled and followed the beast.

Note the following seven things this passage reveals:

1. The Antichrist is a man who rises out of the masses of people, represented by the sea.

2. The Antichrist will have dominion over certain

nations in Europe, Africa and the Middle East. The seven heads and 10 horns represent various national entities.

3. The Antichrist is called a "beast" who will look like a man with animal instincts. The leopard, the bear and the lion are carnivores.

4. The Antichrist will be possessed and controlled by Satan, the dragon.

5. The Antichrist will have great authority.

6. The Antichrist will be nearly assassinated but will be miraculously healed.

7. The Antichrist will be hailed by the whole world as a miracle worker.

Look also at Daniel 7:25-27.

He shall speak pompous words against the Most High, shall persecute the saints of the Most High, and shall intend to change times and law. Then the saints shall be given into his hand for a time and times and half a time. But the court shall be seated, and they shall take away his dominion, to consume and destroy it forever. Then the kingdom and dominion, and the greatness of the kingdoms under the whole heaven, shall be given to the people, the saints of the Most High. His kingdom is an everlasting kingdom, and all dominions shall serve and obey Him.

We must remember the following truths:

1. The Antichrist's kingdom will devour the whole earth.

2. He will blaspheme the most high God and persecute the people of God.

3. The Antichrist will remake history.

4. God's kingdom will triumph over the Antichrist.

Who is the Antichrist?

The Bible gives us some very important details about what this person will represent. We know that the Antichrist is a human being, given over to Satan. We also know he will be a prominent political figure. Daniel 8:20-22 and 11:40, 41 seem to indicate that he will arise out of Media-Persia, which could be our modern Iraq or Iran, or Greece:

The ram which you saw, having the two horns—they are the kings of Media and Persia. And the male goat is the kingdom of Greece. The large horn that is between its eyes is the first king. As for the broken horn and the four that stood up in its place, four kingdoms shall arise out of that nation, but not with its power.... "At the time of the end the king of the South shall attack him; and the king of the North shall come against him like a whirlwind, with chariots, horsemen, and with many ships; and he shall enter the countries, overwhelm them, and pass through. He shall also enter the Glorious Land, and many countries shall be overthrown; but these shall escape from his hand: Edom, Moab, and the prominent people of Ammon."

This passage teaches us that the Antichrist will spare Edom, Moab and Ammon. This area is the modern-day Jordan. He will conquer Egypt, Ethiopia and Libya, as well as Israel.

Many are aware of the Greek influences that were present among the Palestinian Arabs in the Holy Land. The Greek Orthodox Church is the largest Christian group in that part of the world. It seems to me that the Antichrist could possibly be a European-influenced and educated Arab.

Will the Antichrist be a Muslim? Yes, but as stated earlier, he will eventually forsake Islam and declare himself to be God or Allah.

Then the king shall do according to his own will: he shall exalt and magnify himself above every god, shall speak blasphemies against the God of gods, and shall prosper till the wrath has been accomplished; for what has been determined shall be done. He shall regard neither the God of his fathers nor the desire of women, nor regard any god; for he shall exalt himself above them all. But in their place he shall honor a god of fortresses; and a god which his fathers did not know he shall honor with gold and silver, with precious stones and pleasant things (11:36-38).

Notice clearly that the Antichrist believes himself to be God. He will blaspheme all gods, including Allah and the true and living God! Further, he is controlled by and worships Satan. He will deceive religious people and only at the end will he reveal his Satanic designs. His betrayal of Israel will be why Islam will join with him. Their hatred of Israel will cause them to deny even the basic confessions of their faith. They will deny the Son of God and will embrace the sons of the devil.

Antichrist 's Ultimate Deception

Second Thessalonians 2:1-12 gives us further insight.

Now we beseech you, brethren, by the coming of our Lord Jesus Christ, and by our gathering together unto him, that ye be not soon shaken in mind, or be troubled, neither by spirit, nor by word, nor by letter as from us, as that the day of Christ is at hand. Let no man deceive you by any means: for that day shall not come, except there come a falling away first, and that man of sin be revealed, the son of perdition; who opposeth and exalteth himself above all that is called God, or that is worshipped; so that he as God sitteth in the temple of God, shewing himself that he is God. Remember ye not, that, when I was yet with you, I told you these things? And now ye know what with-holdeth that he might be revealed in his time. For the mystery of iniquity doth already work: only he who now letteth will let, until he be taken out of the way. And then shall that Wicked be revealed, whom the Lord shall consume with the spirit of his mouth, and shall destroy with the brightness of his coming: Even him, whose coming is after the working of Satan with all power and signs and lying wonders, and with all deceivableness of unrighteousness in them that per-ish; because they received not the love of the truth, that they might be saved. And for this cause God shall send them strong delusion, that they should believe a lie: that they all might be damned who believed not the truth, but had pleasure in unrighteousness (KJV).

Notice that the Antichrist is the son of perdition. He is the devil incarnate. He claims to be God and dares to blaspheme the true God. He comes as a miracle worker, deceiving and damning the souls of men. He will use a mark to control all of humanity.

He causes all, both small and great, rich and poor, free and slave, to receive a mark on their right hand or on their foreheads, and that no one may buy or sell except one who has the mark or the name of the beast, or the number of his name (Revelation 13:16, 17).

Conclusion

I do not believe the Antichrist is Osama bin Laden or Saddam Hussein. I feel he has not yet been revealed. A man of Arab origin, trained in Western culture and Greek philosophy, will come forth. He will be ecumenical, bringing all religions together. As the son of Satan, he will claim to be God. He will deceive the population of the earth, all who are left after the Rapture. In the end, he will be destroyed at the coming of Jesus!

7
How the Church Hinders the Return of Christ

I n troubled times, fear and oppression can take hold
of God's people. It was so even in Biblical days.
The prophet Isaiah saw the struggles and needs of his
nation, and his heart was moved for the plight of his
people:

> But this is a people robbed and plundered; all of them
> are snared in holes, and they are hidden in prison
> houses; they are for prey, and no one delivers; for
> plunder, and no one says, "Restore!" Who among you
> will give ear to this? Who will listen and hear for the
> time to come? (Isaiah 42:22, 23).

Read also Acts 3:19-21:

> Repent therefore and be converted, that your sins
> may be blotted out, so that times of refreshing may

come from the presence of the Lord, and that He may send Jesus Christ, who was preached to you before, whom heaven must receive until the times of restoration of all things, which God has spoken by the mouth of all His holy prophets since the world began.

This passage tells us clearly that Jesus will not come back until the prophetic word spoken about the church is fulfilled. The bride must be prepared for the coming of her Beloved. There are "times and seasons" related to Jesus' coming.

First Thessalonians 5:1 says: "But concerning the times and the seasons, brethren, you have no need that I should write to you."

A season called "times of refreshing . . . from the presence of the Lord" (Acts 3:19) is near! The end-time church will treasure the presence of Jesus above all. Before the Rapture, there must be a restoration of the church!

Restoring a house is an ordeal. Many months of planning, construction and changing take place before the house can be fully occupied. God is in the process of preparing a house for His coming.

Hebrews 3:6 says Christ is "a Son over His own house, whose house we are if we hold fast the confidence and the rejoicing of the hope firm to the end." Jesus is the High Priest over the house. He invites us into His presence. Listen to His invitation in 10:19-25:

Therefore, brethren, having boldness to enter the Holiest by the blood of Jesus, by a new and living way which He consecrated for us, through the veil, that is, His flesh, and having a High Priest over the house of God, let us draw near with a true heart in full assurance of faith, having our hearts sprinkled from an evil conscience and our bodies washed with pure water. Let us hold fast the confession of our hope without wavering, for He who promised is faithful. And let us consider one another in order to stir up love and good works, not forsaking the assembling of ourselves together, as is the manner of some, but exhorting one another, and so much the more as you see the Day approaching.

As we go into this house:

- We enter by the blood.

- We go through the veil.

- We can draw near.

- We must hold fast!

- We must consider one another.

- We should not forsake the assembly.

The house must be restored before Jesus can return. We must grow more faithful as we see the day of His return approaching!

God has dealt with humanity in three categories: the Jew, the Gentile and the church of God.

"Give no offense, either to the Jews or to the Greeks or to the church of God" (1 Corinthians 10:32).

Today the Jews are restored to their homeland. The Gentile world has united in the European Union, an entity larger than the U.S., Japan and Russia combined. The only "unrestored" group is the church. What must the church become?

The Church: A Place of God's Presence

God is at work making poems of glory out of aliens, strangers, the hopeless and those who are lost. "For we are His workmanship, created in Christ Jesus for good works, which God prepared beforehand that we should walk in them" (Ephesians 2:10).

God's purpose is to remove every boundary and make one *new* man out of us all: ". . . having abolished in His flesh the enmity, that is, the law of commandments contained in ordinances, so as to create in Himself one new man from the two, thus making peace" (Ephesians 2:15). God will move in this new body, making it His holy habitation! The word *habitation* comes from the Greek word *katoikeo*, which means "to reside permanently, to inhabit." In order for God to make this move, He must restore the house!

Now, therefore, you are no longer strangers and foreigners, but fellow citizens with the saints and members of the household of God, having been built on
the foundation of the apostles and prophets, Jesus
Christ Himself being the chief corner stone, in whom
the whole building, being joined together, grows into
a holy temple in the Lord, in whom you also are being
built together for a dwelling place of God in the Spirit
(vv. 19-22).

The Church: A Place of God's Praise

In Matthew 16:18, Jesus said, "I will build my
church." Paul further said in 1 Corinthians 3:9: "You
are God's building." Peter added, "You also, as living
stones, are built up a spiritual house" (1 Peter 2:5).

The Book of Acts gives us the same promise:
"After this I will return and will rebuild the tabernacle
of David, which has fallen down; I will rebuild its
ruins, and I will set it up" (15:16).

This is a startling fulfillment of Amos 9:11: "On
that day I will raise up the tabernacle of David, which
has fallen down, and repair its damages; I will raise up
its ruins, and rebuild it as in the days of old."

In fact, Amos 9 plainly describes what will be happening among all of the three groupings God said
would be on the earth in the end times. "I will bring

back the captives of My people Israel; they shall build the waste cities and inhabit them; they shall plant vineyards and drink wine from them; they shall also make gardens and eat fruit from them" (v. 14).

The church will be restored to its glory as "in the days of old" (v. 11). The nation of Israel will be touched by a restored church. " 'That they may possess the remnant of Edom, and all the Gentiles who are called by My name,' says the Lord who does this thing" (v. 12).

End-time events will occur when the Jew has been brought back, the Gentile world is united, and the church is experiencing revival and prosperity. "Behold, the days are coming . . . When the plowman shall overtake the reaper, and the treader of grapes him who sows seed; the mountains shall drip with sweet wine, and all the hills shall flow with it" (v. 13).

The church will be the tabernacle of David! David's tabernacle was a tent pitched on Mount Zion. To that place, David brought the ark of the covenant. He brought up God's precious mercy seat with dancing, singing, instrumental music and unprecedented giving.

> And so it was, when those bearing the ark of the Lord had gone six paces, that he sacrificed oxen and fatted sheep. Then David danced before the Lord with all his might; and David was wearing a linen ephod. So David and all the house of Israel brought up the ark

of the Lord with shouting and with the sound of the trumpet. Now as the ark of the Lord came into the City of David, Michal, Saul's daughter, looked through a window and saw King David leaping and whirling before the Lord; and she despised him in her heart (2 Samuel 6:13-16).

David set the ark in the tent with no veil shielding it! For 40 years, day and night, there was singing, clapping, hand raising, dancing and music taking place for the glory of God.

The Church: A Place of God's Peace

Ephesians 2:14-22 makes this promise:

For He Himself is our peace, who has made both one, and has broken down the middle wall of separation, having abolished in His flesh the enmity, that is, the law of commandments contained in ordinances, so as to create in Himself one new man from the two, thus making peace, and that He might reconcile them both to God in one body through the cross, thereby putting to death the enmity. And He came and preached peace to you who were afar off and to those who were near. For through Him we both have access by one Spirit to the Father. Now, therefore, you are no longer strangers and foreigners, but fellow citizens with the saints and members of the household of God, having been built on the foundation of the apostles and prophets, Jesus Christ Himself being the chief corner stone, in whom the whole building, being joined together, grows into a holy temple in the Lord, in whom you also are being built together for a dwelling place of God in the Spirit.

This is the ideal—God wants the church to be one "new man." This speaks of unity. All that divided us in terms of race, culture and gender vanishes in that type of unity!

First must come a unity of the Spirit, as Ephesians 4:3 states: ". . . endeavoring to keep the unity of the Spirit in the bond of peace."

Next, Jesus pours out the gifts of the Spirit in verses 7-12:

But to each one of us grace was given according to the measure of Christ's gift. Therefore He says: "When He ascended on high, he led captivity captive, and gave gifts to men." (Now this, "He ascended"— what does it mean but that He also first descended into the lower parts of the earth? He who descended is also the One who ascended far above all the heavens, that He might fill all things.) And He Himself gave some to be apostles, some prophets, some evangelists, and some pastors and teachers, for the equipping of the saints for the work of ministry, for the edifying of the body of Christ.

The anointed, equipped church becomes the growing church ". . . from whom the whole body, joined and knit together by what every joint supplies, according to the effective working by which every part does its share, causes growth of the body for the edifying of itself in love" (4:16).

In the Old Testament, ideal unity is pictured in the anointing of the high priest Aaron:

> Behold, how good and how pleasant it is for brethren to dwell together in unity! It is like the precious oil upon the head, running down on the beard, the beard of Aaron, running down on the edge of his garments. It is like the dew of Hermon, descending upon the mountains of Zion; for there the Lord commanded the blessing—life forevermore (Psalm 133:1-3).

Here is the place of commanded blessings. Here is a church with no walls, flowing in unity. This is the church prepared for rapture!

The Church: Prosperity Restored by God

The church will not leave this earth poor and homeless. She will have a material prosperity. In Amos 9:12, the harvest was promised. When the walls of Jerusalem were rebuilt and restored, God took the burden of debt off the people and gave them back what was theirs.

Restore now to them, even this day, their lands, their vineyards, their olive groves, and their houses, also a hundredth of the money and the grain, the new wine and the oil, that you have charged them. So they said, "We will restore it, and will require nothing from them; we will do as you say." Then I called the priests, and required an oath from them that they would do according to this promise (Nehemiah 5:11, 12).

Note also this promise in Joel 2:23-25:

Be glad then, you children of Zion, and rejoice in the Lord your God; for He has given you the former rain faithfully, and He will cause the rain to come down for you—the former rain, and the latter rain in the first month. The threshing floors shall be full of wheat, and the vats shall overflow with new wine and oil. So I will restore to you the years that the swarming locust has eaten, the crawling locust, the consuming locust, and the chewing locust, my great army which I sent among you.

The church will also know a physical prosperity. God will release the healing gifts to the church in the last days as Isaiah prophesied: "I have seen his ways, and will heal him; I will also lead him, and restore comforts to him and to his mourners" (57:18).

And in Jeremiah 30:17 the Lord promises, "I will

restore health to you and heal you of your wounds . . . Because they called you an outcast saying: 'This is Zion; no one seeks her' "

Finally, God will also grant the church a spiritual prosperity in these last days. David prayed, "Restore to me the joy of Your salvation, and uphold me by Your generous Spirit" (Psalm 51:12). The joy of the Lord will testify of God's kingdom breaking through as the apostle Paul describes in Romans 14:17: "For the kingdom of God is not eating and drinking, but righteousness and peace and joy in the Holy Spirit."

Conclusion

The promise of David's Tabernacle and its restoration in the last days also includes the harvest of souls! A restored church is the place where God lives, where He is praised, where there is real unity, and where there is commanded blessing. In these last days, we will prosper and have the resources to reach the waiting harvest.

8
How to Escape the Coming Terror

D uring World War II, a submarine sank off the coast of England. It took some time for the sub to be located. When the divers arrived at the sub, they heard a faint tapping. Listening, they recognized a Morse code message: "Is there any hope? Is there any hope?"

This is the question many honest people are asking today. Science has failed as a messiah; our world grows bigger and hungrier every day. While speaking of peace, nations are arming themselves to the hilt. Political promises are rampant, while behind closed doors, the experts admit that economic, moral and social problems are insurmountable.

In affluent America, the literature, music and dramatic arts teach a degraded philosophy of life that sees no hope. Even in the framework of the Christian church, many of our people are weak and faithless when facing crisis. As never before, the church and the world need to hear the message of the crucified, risen, ascended and returning Lord!

Paul faced a group of Christians at Thessalonica who had grown confused about end-time events. The results of this confusion can be summed up in these words found in 1 Thessalonians 4:13: *ignorance, sorrow* and *hopelessness*. A misunderstanding about death, eternal life and the Second Coming can cause grief among Christians. Paul understood that ignorance of the Word of God on this subject could lead to sorrow in the face of death, and finally, a state of hopelessness.

This group of Christians had no revelation on what happens if a person dies before the coming of Christ. They feared that their loved ones who died simply forfeited their place in the kingdom of heaven. Consequently, they sorrowed and felt a sense of hopelessness. Today, many believe that the church will go through the Great Tribulation.

There are six reasons why I do not believe that the church will face the Great Tribulation:

1. The church is not mentioned as being on the earth during the Great Tribulation. You will search in vain for the church after Revelation 4:1 until the descent of the New Jerusalem. The church has certainly faced persecution and trouble over the

years, and this will continue, but the Great Tribulation is not for the church.

2. The church is not "appointed unto wrath" (see 1 Thessalonians 5:9).

3. The church is to be "gathered together unto Him . . ." (2 Thessalonians 2:1). The word gathered comes from the Greek word, *episunoge*, which means "to collect completely and bring all to one place."

4. The fact that the church is to depart before the Antichrist is revealed (v. 3).

5. The Old Testament types such as Lot and Enoch picture the Rapture. Lot departed before the fire fell on Sodom (Luke 17). Enoch was raptured before the coming judgment of the Flood.

6. God promises the church a "blessed hope" (Titus 2:13).

The first event that must take place before the day of the Lord comes is called the "falling away" in the original King James Version of the Bible. I believe this translation wasn't very accurate. The basis for this translation lies in the fact that elsewhere in the Bible, a time of great apostasy or "falling away" from true Christian doctrine is prophesied for the time preceding the Lord's return. Although this is true in itself, it is not the meaning of the Greek word found here.

The word translated "falling away" is the Greek word *apostasia*, preceded by the definite article. *Apostasia* has given us our English word *apostasy*, but the word itself simply means "a departure." In a context where the truth or falsity of doctrine is in view, the word would naturally mean "a departure from true doctrine" or "apostasy." But here in 2 Thessalonians 2:3, where the issue is the past or future coming of Jesus Christ for His saints, and where a particular event is specified by the use of the article, the word can also mean "the departure of believers to be with Jesus," or the event we know as the Rapture.

In Kenneth S. Wuest's study, referred to earlier, the following additional facts are elaborated upon. The word *apostasia*, appears in the New Testament only twice. But it is based on the verb *aphistemi*, which occurs 15 times. Eleven times it is translated "depart," never as "a falling away." Unfortunately, most of the English versions follow the leading of the King James Version.

In his book, *The Last and Future World*, Dr. James Boice makes this point:

> It is significant that in the versions that precede the publication of the King James Bible—those of Tyndale (1525), Coverdale (1535), Cranmer (1539), and the Geneva Bible (1560)—the word *apostasia* was translated as departure, and the reference was obviously to the much-anticipated rapture of God's saints.

Evidence That Affirms His Coming

We have confidence that Christ will return! The first evidence appealed to is the supernatural foundation for *our hope*. Christ died so that death might be called "sleep" to those who know Him (1 Corinthians 11:30; 15:51; 1 Thessalonians 4:14). He rose that we might not fear death any longer. If you believe in His death and resurrection, you must also affirm His coming.

In 1 Corinthians 15:12-15, Paul argued that to deny Christ's resurrection is to deny any resurrection from the dead. But to affirm His resurrection is to affirm the resurrection of those who believe on Him. The plan of salvation is incomplete without the resurrection of the saved. If the Head of the church lives, the body of the church must follow.

The Firstfruit, our great Savior the Lord Jesus, has gone on to heaven before us, but the main harvest is to follow. The Jews were commanded to cut the first-ripened grain in their fields, take it to Jerusalem, and lay it upon the altar as a pledge of the coming harvest and a thankful offering to God. At the end of the harvest, they met again in Jerusalem to celebrate the harvest feast.

Our blessed Savior now is the Firstfruit in heaven. He is the pledge of the glorious harvest that, at the end of the age, will leave every old tomb tenantless. He will, in bodily form, gather all of the redeemed and glorified to heaven.

Our Savior conquered death, our foe. When Jesus was taken off the cross and borne to the tomb, death waved its black banner in triumph. I believe sighs could almost be heard among the tombs of the patriarchs, and a wail of woe amid the sepulchers of the dead. Death lifted its scepter as a king without a rival.

Jesus met death in its own territory and permitted Himself to be captured so that He might lead captivity captive. He went with the pale monarch, death, to the silent darkness of the tomb.

But glory to God, He undermined death's strongholds and kindled the star of resurrection in the murky vaults of death. He plucked the sting from death, took the keys, broke the crown, spoiled the monster and came forth as conqueror! So now, because of His finished work, we are conquerors with Him.

Another evidence of His coming is the infallible Word of our God (v. 15). Paul based what he said on the word of the Lord. Jesus himself taught the truth of His return. The blessed hope of our Lord's coming is the stepchild of modern theology. Bible-believing Christians will ever affirm their faith in "that blessed hope and glorious appearing of the great God and our Savior Jesus Christ" (Titus 2:13). Believers need this hope for comfort and strength. It also protects them from the evil doctrines that arise to contradict faith, such as Armstrongism and Jehovah's Witnesses.

Events that Accompany His Coming

> For the Lord Himself will descend from heaven with
> a shout, with the voice of an archangel, and with the
> trumpet of God. And the dead in Christ will rise first.
> Then we who are alive and remain shall be caught up
> together with them in the clouds to meet the Lord in
> the air. And thus we shall always be with the Lord
> (1 Thessalonians 4:16, 17).

The central figure in these verses is the Lord himself. He who had been exalted to the right hand of the Father, the One who holds the highest authority, the highest reputation as the Lord of all, will one day leave His throne and step from the lofty heights of heaven's splendor to descend toward earth.

What a glorious scene that will be! When Peter wrote about the second coming of the Lord, his mind turned to that moment he witnessed on the Mount of Transfiguration. There, through sleepy eyes, they saw the glory of His deity.

> Moreover I will endeavour that ye may be able after
> my decease to have these things always in remem-
> brance. For we have not followed cunningly devised
> fables, when we made known unto you the power and
> coming of our Lord Jesus Christ, but were eyewitness-
> es of his majesty. For he received from God the Father

honour and glory, when there came such a voice to him from the excellent glory, This is my beloved Son, in whom I am well pleased. And this voice which came from heaven we heard, when we were with him in the holy mount (2 Peter 1:15-18, KJV).

After Christ's death, Peter wanted others to know about the great glory of Christ he had witnessed. One day, we will again see that glory. We will hear the shout, the voice of the archangel and the trumpet of God. As angels sang over Christ's birth, so will they accompany His triumphant return to earth. My prayer is that of songwriter Horatio Spafford:

> And Lord, haste the day
> when our faith shall be sight,
> The clouds be rolled back as a scroll;
> The trumpet shall resound,
> and the Lord shall descend;
> Even so, it is well with my soul.

The second event that accompanies Christ's coming is the miracle of resurrection. When Jesus descends, I believe the shout will come from His own lips. As the Lord of both the dead and the living, He will shout into the tombs of the multitudes who knew Him as Savior, "Come forth!" The voice of the Savior will resound through the length and breadth of death's empire and bring it crashing down.

"Come forth!" from the Creator himself will bring the ashes and dust of those who knew Him to remembrance. At His command, from the sea and from the land, their bodies are resurrected and immortalized just as His glorious body—united with the conscious spirits of those saints. What a glorious day when the winding sheets of desert sands give up their dead, when the oceans of the world swell and heave multiplied thousands out their watery depths! The battlefields will give up their dead, and graveyards will look like plowed fields. Oh, the glory of that day!

I have a brother and a sister-in-law whom God recently blessed with a son. He looked as though angels had given him the twinkle in his eyes. One day, mysteriously, the tiny baby stopped breathing. I can still see my brother holding the little mittens, and my sister holding the blanket. She said that she would often wake up at night, thinking she felt his little hand. They laid him in a dark coffin, but on that great day of the Lord, they will see their precious little one again!

I stood once as the 21-gun salute sounded and "Taps" was played as the body of a soldier was lowered into a grave. I saw his six children standing nearby and heard the little 5-year-old boy ask his sobbing mother, "When's daddy coming home?"

There will be an eternity for those seemingly unfair tragedies to be righted. The great day of His coming will amend the inequities of life. No matter the tragedy Christians face before death, one day they will be raised whole to meet the Lord. "Weeping may endure for a night, but joy cometh in the morning" (Psalm 30:5, KJV).

This is the event that will dramatically herald the coming of the Lord—the Rapture of the church, which the apostle Paul spoke of in 1 Corinthians 15. He called the Rapture a *musterion* in the Greek, something "brought out in the open." Those who are alive at the Lord's coming will "be changed . . . in the twinkling of an eye" (vv. 51, 52).

The voice of the archangel will cry, "Behold, the bridegroom cometh" (Matthew 23:5, KJV). Then in a flash, swiftly and irresistibly, the saints will be translated into glory. The phrase, *caught up in the clouds* (1 Thessalonians 9:17), is filled with meaning. It was the cloud of *shekinah* glory that took away our Lord in Acts 1:9: "Now when He had spoken these things, while they watched, He was taken up, and a cloud received Him out of their sight."

He will come back in the clouds as promised in Matthew 24:30: "Then the sign of the Son of Man will appear in heaven, and then all the tribes of the earth will mourn, and they will see the Son of Man coming on the clouds of heaven with power and great glory."

His glory at the transfiguration included a voice from

a cloud. One day, like Enoch and Elijah, a whole generation of believers will be transferred to glory without facing death. We shall be caught up into the *shekinah* glory itself. Oh blessed hope! Perhaps today . . .

> A moment more, and then away.
> Caught up in the clouds to be with Him
> Beyond the reach of conflicts grim,
> Of disappointments, pain and tears.
> Oh, blessed hope, the rapture nears!
>
> —Anne Lind-Woodworth

Think of the marvel of the reunion on that day! My great aunt planned a reunion for our whole family on a beautiful spring Saturday several years ago. Sadly, my uncle John died three days before the scheduled event. I remember my aunt saying, "We'll have to call off the reunion." I told her we were not calling it off; we were simply postponing it for awhile!

The Expectancy of His Coming

Having looked at the evidence that affirms Christ's coming and the events that accompany His coming, we should consider our anticipation as we await His return! How should we act as we watch for His return?

First, we should examine ourselves. In 1 Thessalonians 4:17: "Then we who are alive and remain shall be caught up together with them in the clouds to meet the Lord in the air. And thus we shall always be with the Lord."

We find there the word *meet*. This word is used as an official greeting, such as a king would give to a returning ambassador. As Christ's ambassadors, we can be sure He will examine us to see how well we have represented Him. You will not give an account to your denomination, to your church, to your spouse, or to your parents, but to the Lord himself. As we prepare for His return, we should search our lives for anything that needs to be brought into line with His Word and will.

Next, we should prepare for celebration! That same word *meet* in our passage can also mean the official gathering at a wedding. As Christ's bride, the church awaits the coming of the Bridegroom. In John 14, He told us that He was going away to prepare the Father's house and then He is coming back for us.

In modern weddings, we have reversed it. Today most bridegrooms await the bride at the end of the altar. I remember how lovely my wife looked on our day. She walked gracefully down the aisle, wearing a beautiful white gown covered with over 3,000 seed pearls in exquisite finery. Her face was veiled, but then uncovered. What a happy moment!

So shall we be reunited with our Bridegroom and look upon His face in joy and wonder and celebration!

Conclusion

A historic engagement of war occurred in Operation Thunderbolt, when Israeli commandos flew a secret route and swiftly landed at Entebbe, Uganda. They overcame their enemies who had hijacked a plane there, rescued the prisoners being held, and flew home to safety. When they arrived home, it was a scene of great rejoicing!

One day the Captain of our salvation will stand, give the shout and signal the archangel to sound the trumpet. "Operation Rapture" will commence!

Jesus will descend into the realm of death and despair to rescue us. On the wings of His glory, He will carry us aloft to be with Him. What a day of rejoicing! There will be a grand celebration on that day. Isaiah caught the spirit of this glorious future:

He will swallow up death forever, and the Lord God will wipe away tears from all faces; the rebuke of His people he will take away from all the earth; for the Lord has spoken. And it will be said in that day: "Behold, this is our God; we have waited for Him, and He will save us. This is the Lord; we have waited for Him; we will be glad and rejoice in His salvation" (25:8, 9).

9
When Will Armageddon Begin?

T hough humanity has longed and sought for peace, war has been a legacy. In one of the earliest of historical records, a Sumerian bas-relief—estimated to be from 3000 B.C.—depicts soldiers fighting. Wars fill the chronicles of ancient civilizations such as Egypt, Babylon, Assyria and Israel. Conflicts like the Peloponnesian War and Battle of Carchemish stand out. World empires sought and won power through war.

Rome made war an engine of prosperity. In the 17th century, the Thirty Years War ravaged Europe. Britain and Spain fought off and on for more than a century. World War I cost approximately 37 million lives, and World War II cost nearly 17 million lives. We have lived through the Korean War, the Vietnam War, and the continuing conflict in the Middle East. Now we see small but violent conflicts all over the world. In the midst of this, our hearts long for peace.

The world is headed for a final conflagration. We have clear descriptions of this war in Revelation, Daniel and Ezekiel.

The Last War—Armageddon

The final battle of mankind will reveal four world powers clashing over the Middle East. Revelation 6 describes the four horsemen, the second of which is the red horse of war. In 9:16, we also find a description of an army of 200 million crossing a dried-up Euphrates River into the Middle East.

Revelation 11:9 describes the claiming back of the earth by its owner and Creator, the Lord Jesus. Death and destruction will be the opening volleys of that last war, and it will be located at a place called *Armageddon*.

> Then the sixth angel poured out his bowl on the great river Euphrates, and its water was dried up, so that the way of the kings from the east might be prepared. And I saw three unclean spirits like frogs coming out of the mouth of the dragon, out of the mouth of the beast, and out of the mouth of the false prophet. For they are spirits of demons, performing signs, which go out to the kings of the earth and of the whole

world, to gather them to the battle of that great day of God Almighty. "Behold, I am coming as a thief. Blessed is he who watches, and keeps his garments, lest he walk naked and they see his shame." And they gathered them together to the place called in Hebrew, Armageddon (16:12-16).

Where is Armageddon?

The name *Armageddon* comes from two words in Hebrew—*Har*, meaning mountain, and *Megiddo*, the name of an ancient city. When one stands on the mountain near Megiddo, he overlooks the plain of Esdraelon, Valley of Jezreel.

Napoleon looked at this valley in his time and declared it to be "the world's greatest natural battle-field." A walk through any history book confirms this, for Megiddo has been the site of many battles.

Thutmose III	1479 B.C.	Egypt
Ramses VI	c.1170 B.C.	Egypt
Sargon II	720 B.C.	Assyria
Sennacherib	701 B.C.	Assyria
Pharaoh Necho	609 B.C.	Egypt
Nebuchadnezzar	586 B.C.	Babylon
Alexander the Great	332 B.C.	Greece

Antiochus Epiphanies	c.168 B.C.	Greece
Pompei	63 B.C.	Rome
Titus	A.D. 70	Rome
Omar II	A.D. 637	Islam
Stoicous	A.D. 909	France
Saladin	A.D. 1187	Islam
Ottoman	A.D. 1516	Islam

Besides these wars and conflicts, the valley of Jezreel was also the place where fire fell from heaven at the prayer of Elijah. And fire will fall again!

Several years ago, I stood with a tour group at Mount Carmel and saw black jets streaking overhead and landing in the valley of Jezreel, at Armageddon. As they landed, I noticed that they disappeared under ground! I was told that an extensive military complex exists there! The great battlefield stands ready for end-time events!

Great Armies United

Many armies will be present at the great battle of Armageddon. Daniel 7:7, 8 and Revelation 13 discuss the Antichrist. They indicate a revived Roman Empire, a confederacy that is now in place in Europe. Daniel 11:21, 36-39 speaks of the acts of the Antichrist as he leads the western confederacy.

And in his place shall arise a vile person, to whom they will not give the honor of royalty; but he shall come in peaceably, and seize the kingdom by intrigue. Then the king shall do according to his own will: he shall exalt and magnify himself above every god, shall speak blasphemies against the God of gods, and shall prosper till the wrath has been accomplished; for what has been determined shall be done. He shall regard neither the God of his fathers nor the desire of women, nor regard any god; for he shall exalt himself above them all. But in their place he shall honor a god of fortresses; and a god which his fathers did not know he shall honor with gold and silver, with precious stones and pleasant things. Thus he shall act against the strongest fortresses with a foreign god, which he shall acknowledge, and advance its glory; and he shall cause them to rule over many, and divide the land for gain.

Also present in that great battle will be the king of the North. Ezekiel 38:1-3 seems to tell us that this power is Russia. Meshech and Tubal, the cities named in the passage, are ancient names of Moscow and Tobolsk. Both Herodotus and Josephus, ancient historians, point to these ancient tribes as migrating to Russia.

Furthermore, *Rosh* translates literally as "chief prince" in the King James Version. The *New King James Version, New American Standard Version, New*

English Bible and the *Jerusalem Bible* all translate this verse to read "Prince of Rosh." Gesenius, in his Hebrew lexicon, states that Rosh is most likely the Russians.

Allies of this power of the north include Ethiopia (Luz), Persia (Iran and Iraq), North Africa (Put), Turkey (Togarmah) and Germany (Gomer). Russia will be destroyed on the mountains for Israel. According to Ezekiel 38 and 39, another army present will be that of the king of the south. Daniel 11:40 indicates that the king of the south is Egypt—a power that will actually initiate the battle of Armageddon.

In addition, we find that the king of the east will take its place in this end battle (see Daniel 11:44; Revelation 9:16, 16:12). This power could be China, Japan, India or an alliance of these nations. This army of the king of the east will number 200 million!

The Fighting at Armageddon

What will be the nature of the fighting at this historic battle?

1. Egypt will move on Israel, according to Daniel 11:40, in defiance of the treaty of Israel with the Antichrist.

2. Russia will ally with Egypt and invade Israel (Daniel 11:41).

3. Russia will break her agreement with Egypt and will march through Israel to capture Egypt.

4. Russia will be destroyed on the mountain of Israel.

5. European powers (most likely including the United States) will move into the vacuum created by Russia at their defeat. The Western confederation will be used of God to destroy Russia, and new-world domination looms before Antichrist.

6. All armies will be marshaled to Armageddon (see Revelation 16:14-16). The eastern confederation of the "king of the east," possibly a union of Japan, China and India will come to fight the Antichrist to try and gain world domination. The world will explode in war (see Revelation 16:18-21).

The Final Chapter of the Great Battle

At this dark hour, with all the world waging war against the Antichrist, another king and invasion force will enter the picture—the King of kings and Lord of lords, the King of heaven! Revelation 19:11 describes the coming of Jesus to reign on earth: "Now I saw heaven opened, and behold, a white horse. And He who sat on him was called Faithful and True, and in righteousness He judges and makes war."

Jesus ends the battle with His conquering word! The extent of His glorious victory will be addressed in the next chapter. But dear reader, you need to be on the winning side. You can escape Armageddon! You can trust King Jesus as your Savior and be sealed against that Day of Judgment.

10
Who Is the King of Glory?

A t this point in our study, the last world war is raging. The world religious system has collapsed. World social and economic systems have collapsed. The beast (Antichrist), his armies, and an army of 200 million from the east are marching into a mighty clash. It seems the only world system that remains is a military system. Men's hearts have become so full of hatred and greed that all that is left of societal order is a military machine.

At the height of this great confrontation at Armageddon comes a heavenly interruption—the return of Jesus Christ. Let us look together at six aspects of His arrival.

Christ's Appearing

The Lord's return will be in glorious contrast to

His first coming. This world welcomed Jesus in a stable and then said farewell to Him on a cross. He appeared as man and Son of Man. He was fully human and fully divine. His humanity was His manifestation. He came unknown, born in a small village and limited in His travels. His fame only spread abroad after He left the earth.

At His second coming, things will be different! According to Philippians 2, Jesus took the journey downward from glory to death on the cross. After His resurrection, He made the journey back upward. So at His second coming, His deity will again be manifest. Every eye will see Him, and His appearing will be glorious. Heaven will be opened. For the first time, the natural eye of man will see the eternal glory of God.

Christ will ride into the midst of Armageddon, seated upon a white horse. The white steed symbolizes His right as conquering King. He will come in righteousness to judge and make war. His cause is right. His judgments, though terrible, are just and deserved. His eyes will be a flame of fire. His scorching gaze will sear the wickedness of man.

The Apparel of the King

The Bible is detailed in its description of Christ's raiment at His return. Revelation 19:12, 13 says that He will wear a crown. The word used is *diadem*, which indicates a crown of imperial dignity. His crown of authority stands over every other authority. He will be visibly crowned with glory.

The clothing the King will wear is also striking. His robe is dipped in blood. This clothing reminds us of the suffering, conquering Messiah described in Isaiah. Christ wears blood-stained garments to symbolize two things: His shed blood for the lost and the blood of those who have rejected His offer of pardon.

The first time Jesus came, His garments were stained with His own blood—blood shed for our salvation, precious and life-giving. He comes from the victory of Calvary, blood-stained but victorious, now to shed the blood of those who refused salvation.

The Army of the King

The first time Christ came, though heralded by angels, He had to face the bitter cup alone. At His return, He will bring the fruits of victory! Accompanying Him, along with the holy angels, will be an army of saints. In fact, all who are saved will return with Him as coregents.

Notice that the dress of the army in Revelation 19:14 is exactly the same as the bride in verse 8: "And the armies in heaven, clothed in fine linen, white and clean, followed Him on white horses." We are going to accompany Christ at His glorious entrance! Jude 14 confirms this wonderful hope: "Now Enoch, the seventh from Adam, prophesied about these men also, saying, 'Behold, the Lord comes with ten thousands of His saints.' "

The Attack of the Returning King

At His first coming, Jesus suffered the attacks of men and of Satan. At His return, He will not be on the defensive, but on the offensive. He will attack with the army of the faithful. He will attack with a certainty of victory. In fact, so certain is the victory that all scavenger birds are told to get ready for a gruesome feast (vv. 17, 18).

The King of kings will attack all the armies gathered together by the beast and Satan. The Lord will attack with but one weapon—the Word: "Now out of His mouth goes a sharp sword, that with it He should strike the nations. And He Himself will rule them with a rod of iron. He Himself treads the winepress of the fierceness and wrath of Almighty God" (v. 15).

The weapon of the Word will render the battle over in seconds and will make all human weaponry useless. Isn't it sad that we do not use this spiritual weapon more now! Hebrews 4:12 declares that God's Word is our strongest weapon: "For the word of God is living and powerful, and sharper than any two-edged sword, piercing even to the division of soul and spirit, and of joints and marrow, and is a discerner of the thoughts and intents of the heart."

The King's Anger

Jesus is coming back to execute wrath and judgment on an ungodly world. When He came the first time, He stood before men to be judged. But at this return, men will stand in judgment before Him!

The King's anger will be kindled. The day of vengeance that has been stored up will arrive. Wrath will have its payday. Second Thessalonians 1:4-12 describes both the terror and the justice of that awful hour.

So that we ourselves boast of you among the churches of God for your patience and faith in all your persecutions and tribulations that you endure, which is manifest evidence of the righteous judgment of God, that you may be counted worthy of the kingdom of God, for which you also suffer; since it is a righteous thing with God to repay with tribulation those who trouble you, and to give you who are troubled rest with us when the Lord Jesus is revealed from heaven with His mighty angels, in flaming fire taking vengeance on those who do not know God, and on those who do not obey the gospel of our Lord Jesus Christ. These shall be punished with everlasting destruction from the presence of the Lord and from the glory of His power, when He comes, in that Day, to be glorified in His saints and to be admired among all those who believe, because our testimony among you was believed. Therefore we also pray always for

you that our God would count you worthy of this call-
ing, and fulfill all the good pleasure of His goodness
and the work of faith with power, that the name of our
Lord Jesus Christ may be glorified in you, and you in
Him, according to the grace of our God and the Lord
Jesus Christ.

Furthermore, He will judge the beast and the false
prophet. Revelation 19:20 says, "And the beast was
taken, and with him the false prophet that wrought
miracles before him, with which he deceived them
that had received the mark of the beast, and them that
worshipped his image. These both were cast alive into
a lake of fire burning with brimstone" (KJV).

The word *taken* indicates being "snatched up," like
a cat takes a mouse or like a lion takes an antelope.
These evil beings will be snatched up and cast into the
lake of fire.

The Authority of the Returning King

Before Jesus left this earth, He taught us to pray
"Thy Kingdom come . . ." (Matthew 6:10; Luke 11:2,
KJV). Indeed, His kingdom comes invisibly as souls
crown Him Lord of their hearts. But His kingdom will
come visibly when He returns. First Timothy 6:14
reminds us to "keep this commandment without spot,
blameless until our Lord Jesus Christ's appearing."

Christ will indeed be Lord over all. At present, the Deceiver is holding sway. One day our Lord will rule over it all in great power and glory.

Conclusion

In Philippians 2 we read that "every knee shall bow and every tongue shall confess that Jesus Christ is Lord." In our day, there are a few who are bowing the knee to Jesus, but in that day, all the earth will bow.

On which side of eternity will you bow? Will you wait until then and hear the awful words, "Depart from Me, you cursed, into the everlasting fire" (Matthew 25:41)? While grace and hope still abound, embrace the King of kings.

11

Heaven Holds Court

Perhaps you have had to appear before a judge for some legal infraction or issue. Perhaps the traffic ticket you received requires you to appear in court. As the day approaches, you fearfully go over the details again and again to be sure you relate the truth and only the truth.

If we place that much concern and importance on minor days of judgment in our earthly world, think how much more seriously we should consider the coming day of judgment that heaven is preparing!

Most solemnly the Bible warns, "It is appointed for men to die once, but after this the judgment" (Hebrews 9:27). The word *judgment* comes from the Greek word *krisis*. Our English word *crisis* comes from this word. It is a time of great importance. A day is coming when the lost dead of all the ages stand before God—the Great White Throne Judgment.

Understand that this final judgment stands apart from other judgments discussed in Scripture. Scripture tells us of several other judgments:

1. The judgment of the believer's sins at the cross through the shedding of Christ's blood

2. The judgment seat of Christ, taking place immediately after the Rapture of the church, which is a judgment of reward, not of salvation

3. The judgment of Israel and the nations of the world (see Matthew 25:1-46), which takes place following Christ's glorious return at Armageddon, and precedes the millennial reign

4. The judgment of Satan and the fallen angels (see 2 Peter 2:4; Jude 6; Revelation 20:10), after which Satan and all the hosts that follow him will be cast into the lake

5. The Great White Throne Judgment is the last of these judgments. All of them are separate and distinct.

The High Court

The location of the court scene for this final judgment is terrifying. God suspends a Great White Throne. This throne is significant—it is great, indicating power, it is white, indicating holiness; and the fact that it is a throne indicates God's ultimate authority. The lost—dead and alive—will be transported instantly and will stand suspended before the Lord. Both the earth and its atmosphere will experience an intense purging by fire. Second Peter 3:10-13 describes the heavens and the earth on fire:

> But the day of the Lord will come as a thief in the night, in which the heavens will pass away with a great noise, and the elements will melt with fervent heat; both the earth and the works that are in it will be burned up. Therefore, since all these things will be dissolved, what manner of persons ought you to be in holy conduct and godliness, looking for and hastening the coming of the day of God, because of which the heavens will be dissolved, being on fire, and the elements will melt with fervent heat? Nevertheless we, according to His promise, look for new heavens and a new earth in which righteousness dwells.

Homeless in Eternity

The Bible states that for those who were judged, "there was found no place for them" (Revelation 20:11). I believe this refers to the lost. At the judgment, there will be no place to hide. Everything that they lived for will be shown to come to naught. Every monument of man will be dissolved in that day. There is no place to hide in front of the Lord's righteous gaze.

Presiding over this judgment will be God, specifically—the Lord Jesus Christ. Scripture supports this in the following passages:

- John 5:22 says, "the Father . . . hath committed all judgment to the Son" (KJV).

- Paul wrote in Romans 2:16, "God will judge the secrets of men by Jesus Christ."

- In Acts 10:42, Peter preaches, "it is He [Jesus] who was ordained of God to be the Judge of the living and dead."

- Paul declares in Acts 17:31 that "he hath appointed a day, in the which he will judge the world in righteousness by that man whom he hath ordained; whereof he hath given assurance unto all men, in that he hath raised him from the dead."

- Second Timothy 4:1 also states, "the Lord Jesus Christ . . . shall judge the quick and the dead at His appearing" (KJV).

I read the story of a criminal who appeared a second time in court for the same offense. A skillful lawyer had gotten him off the first time; but now, years later, the criminal was back under a similar charge. As the judge came into court, a smile crossed the defendant's face. The judge was the same man who had been his lawyer years before! Confident and cocky, the criminal drifted through the proceedings.

How shocked he was as the verdict was read—not only was he found guilty, but he was also given the most severe sentence possible. Looking up at the judge, his former lawyer, he demanded, "How could you punish me this way?"

The judge replied, "I was once your lawyer, but now I'm your judge and must act differently regarding your actions."

Jesus is your lawyer now, but He will someday be your judge! A summons is issued to every unsaved person. All of the wicked dead stand before God. Not one saved soul will be there. Not one lost person will escape the Great White Throne Judgment. Hebrews 10:26-31 describes the fearful procedures of that day:

> For if we sin willfully after we have received the knowledge of the truth, there no longer remains a sacrifice for sins, but a certain fearful expectation of judgment, and fiery indignation which will devour the adversaries. Anyone who has rejected Moses' law dies without mercy on the testimony of two or three witnesses. Of how much worse punishment, do you suppose, will he be thought worthy who has trampled the Son of God underfoot, counted the blood of the

covenant by which he was sanctified a common thing, and insulted the Spirit of grace? For we know Him who said, "Vengeance is Mine; I will repay," says the Lord. And again, "The Lord will judge His people." It is a fearful thing to fall into the hands of the living God.

The Evidence Presented

At this final courtroom, the books will be opened. From those books, every person's entire life will be judged. As Numbers 32:23 states, "Be sure your sin will find you out." An exact record is being kept. In Amos 8:7, God says, "I will never forget any of their works." God also declared that He "will, by no means clear the guilty" (Exodus 34:7).

Everything done in secret will be brought into the open. Every idle word (Matthew 12:36), all ungodly works (Jude 14, 15), youthful sins (Ecclesiastes 11:9), and all works without exception (12:14) will be judged. Every skeleton will come out of the closet!

Another book will be opened—the Book of Life. It will be checked to see if a person's name appears in it. The Book of Life was written before the world was created and "All who dwell on the earth will worship him, whose names have not been written in the Book of Life of the Lamb slain from the foundation of the world" (Revelation 13:8).

This book contains the names of everyone who would ever live. Names are not written in that book, but they are blotted out. God promises not to blot out the names of the overcomers. "He who overcomes shall be clothed in white garments, and I will not blot out his name from the Book of Life; but I will confess his name before My Father and before His angels" (3:5).

Psalm 69:28 states, "Let them be blotted out of the book of the living and not be written with the righteous."

When a person dies without receiving Christ, he hardens his heart by sinning away his day of grace. At that moment, that person's name is blotted out. God declared, "Whoever hath sinned against me, him will I blot out of my book" (Exodus 32:33). Only the names of the saved remain in that Book of Life. They are enrolled in heaven. Hebrews 12:22, 23 states the following: "But you have come to Mount Zion and to the city of the living God, the heavenly Jerusalem, to an innumerable company of angels, to the general assembly and church of the firstborn who are registered in heaven, to God the Judge of all, to the spirits of just men made perfect."

Everyone has a chance to be saved. When an individual refuses the life offered in Jesus Christ by the cleansing blood, his wicked record remains on the books and his name is blotted out of the Book of Life.

A saved man, however, has his wicked record washed clean by Christ, and his name stands written in glory.

The Verdict of the Court

Guilty! This verdict will strike at the very core of the lost ones standing before God. Many will say, "Lord, Lord" and try to hold up their good works, but it will be too late. Weeping and gnashing of teeth will have begun for an eternity.

Three things fell under the curse of God at the Fall in the Garden of Eden: Satan, the earth and man. Prior to the Great White Throne Judgment, Satan will have been cast into the lake of fire. All members of mankind who did not repent and turn to Christ will pay the price for their rejection.

The sentence for the guilty will be eternity in the lake of fire—a literal second death. All of the lost will be cast alive into the burning flames of the lake of fire. How awful will be the torments of that eternity!

12

Hell: A Reality

T he passages below are the most solemn and fearful words in all of Scripture. Every appeal and warning in Scripture is written to keep persons from experiencing that awful judgment. Because the idea of an eternal torment disturbs the sensitivities of many, one rarely hears a sermon on the subject.

- "And anyone not found written in the Book of Life was cast into the lake of fire" (Revelation 20:15).

- "But the cowardly, unbelieving, abominable, murderers, sexually immoral, sorcerers, idolaters, and all liars shall have their part in the lake which burns with fire and brimstone, which is the second death" (21:8).

- But there shall by no means enter it anything that defiles, or causes an abomination or a lie, but only those who are written in the Lamb's Book of Life" (v. 27).

- "But outside are dogs and sorcerers and sexually immoral and murderers and idolaters, and whoever loves and practices a lie" (22:15).

God set the awful penalty for mankind's sin. "The wages of sin is death" (Romans 6:23). Sin is the river flowing out of hell. Its floods are black and its waves are towering. Old and young alike are disregarding the hour when the payment for their sins will be required.

Scripture exists to warn the lost. Ezekiel 33:11 stands as a vast stoplight, warning, "Turn ye, turn ye . . . why will you die?" (KJV). In Matthew 5:29, 30, Jesus even urges, "And if thy right eye offend thee, pluck it out . . . if thy right hand offend thee, cut it off . . . for it is profitable for thee that one of thy members should perish, and not that thy whole body should be cast into hell."

There is a final place of torment where men must spend an eternity. Four words in the Bible are translated as "hell." Three of these apply directly to a specific location:

1. *Sheol*—This word in the Old Testament translates as "hell" and "grave."

2. *Hades*—This word in the New Testament was

the same. Both the Old and New Testaments refer to this place of the departed. They were general words that referred to the place where both the lost and saved went after death. In Luke 16, we see a description of the realm of departed spirits before the resurrection of Jesus. A place of paradise existed there for the saved, and there were torments for the lost. At His ascension, Jesus took all of paradise on to heaven and left the lost in Hades (torments). One day, this place of torment will be cast into the lake of fire. Man's last enemy and the place of torment will be hurled into the lake of fire.

3. *Gehenna*—This is the word Jesus used for the lake of fire. The word was also used to refer to the place where children were offered to false gods. Later, Jews referred to the city dump of Jerusalem with this word. It was a place where worms crawled and fires burned. It was a place of appalling stench and filth. Jesus pointed to that place and said that would be what the lake of fire would be like.

The lot of a lost man is cast here. At death, his spirit is imprisoned in Hades where it is given a body. He suffers torment until he is released from this prison home to hear the final verdict. At the moment, death and hell are cast into the lake of fire. Then the lost are cast into that awful place forever. The word *final* best describes the eternal state of the lost.

A Final Division of Humanity

Revelation 21:7, 8 affirms the ultimate separation of the lost and the saved: "He who overcomes shall inherit all things, and I will be his God and he shall be My son. But the cowardly, unbelieving, abominable, murderers, sexually immoral, sorcerers, idolaters, and all liars shall have their part in the lake which burns with fire and brimstone, which is the second death."

For the saved, there is a pure river of the water of life. For the lost, there is to be a stagnant lake of fire. The overcomers and the unbelievers must be separated. Verse 27 also affirms that no lost person will ever go into the company of the saved: "But there shall by no means enter it anything that defiles, or causes an abomination or a lie, but only those who are written in the Lamb's Book of Life."

This is a grave warning for us. The lost man will never see his saved wife again. Lost children will never see their believing parents. It will be complete and final. In fact, the lost will be wiped from the memory of the saved.

Final Destiny of Lost Humanity

The word *eternal* is used 69 times in the New Testament. Sixty-two of those times it describes the blessedness of the saved, and seven times it refers to the state of the lost. These passages speak in a most terrifying manner:

Everlasting burning—Isaiah 66:24

Everlasting contempt—Daniel 12:2

Unquenchable fire—Matthew 3:12; Mark 9:43

Everlasting fire—Matthew 25:41

Everlasting punishment—Matthew 25:46

Everlasting destruction—2 Thessalonians 1:9

Tormented forever—Revelation 14:11; 20:10.

The only song in hell has one word, one note, one chorus and one verse. Eternally it rings out in the corridor of the fiery lake—"Forever! Forever!" Out of the realm of the dead it sounds—"Forever! Forever!"

This eternal punishment is also referred to as the second death. "Then Death and Hades were cast into the lake of fire. This is the second death" (Revelation 20:14).

Death is not simply an absence of life. There are three deaths mentioned in Scripture:

1. Physical death—the separation of the spirit of man from his body.

2. Spiritual death—the separation of man from God. This is the state of every lost person until they get saved.

3. Second death—when a person dies physically without being saved. It is the eternal separation of a person from God.

Being in a place without God is awful. The lake of fire is about dying without being destroyed. It is outer darkness with weeping and grinding of teeth. It involves evil and vile companions (see Revelation 21:8; 22:15). There is no goodness there, no fellowship and no joy. It is a literal burning fire. Sin is the spark that kindles the fires of hell. It is a place of haunting memories where lost opportunities will be remembered, and regret and remorse will be constant. No wonder in his epic poem about hell, Dante described the sign over hell's gates: "Abandon all hope, all ye who enter here!"

Conclusion

The lake of fire was prepared for the devil and his angels. It was never meant for humanity. A person chooses to go there when he or she refuses Christ. A person who dies lost and goes to hell does so because of resisting the Bible, the blood of Jesus, the prayer of the saved and the witnessing efforts of the church. How many people will remember their choice, "I chose liquor" or "I chose money" or "I chose popularity with the world."

But there is still hope as the end times approach. There is still time to make a choice. Revelation 20:15 says, "Whosoever was not found written in the book of life is cast into a lake of fire." The decision is yours. You must choose your final and eternal home.

13
What Will Heaven Be Like?

T he word *heaven* in Scripture refers to three things:

1. The atmosphere of earth (Genesis 1:20)

2. The vast outer space, including the moon, star, and galaxies (Psalm 8:3)

3. The dwelling place of God, which is beyond the first two heavens. The throne of God is in this third heaven. It is also called the "heaven of heavens" (see 1 Kings 8:27; 2 Corinthians 12:1-4).

When our Lord ascended on high, He went up through earth's atmosphere and continued up through the starry heavens into the very throne room of God. This dwelling place of God Almighty is referred to in Scripture under many descriptions. Consider these designations:

- Mansion—John 14:2

- Temple—Revelation 21:22

- City—Hebrews 11:10, 16; Revelation 21

- Country—Hebrews 11:16

- Inheritance—1 Peter 1:4

Those who have received Christ's gift of salvation have a future life with both a new heaven and a new earth. Heaven is more than just a place, it is also a state of being. In eternity, whether I am on the new earth or in the heaven of heavens, it will be gladness and glory. Heaven is wherever the grace and glory of Jesus is.

Heaven will be for our resurrected bodies what salvation is to our spirit now. In 2 Corinthians 5:17, Paul says, "If any man be in Christ, he is a new creature: old things are passed away; behold, all things are become new" (KJV). This is exactly what Scripture says heaven will be for us when we are resurrected. Revelation 21:1 says, "the first earth passed away." In verse 4 it states, "The former things are passed away." Later in verse 5, Jesus says, "Behold, I make all things new." Heaven indeed is the place where at last all things are renewed and revitalized.

What Will Not Be in Heaven?

As John wrote the Revelation God gave him about

heaven, he sat exiled on an island, away from all those whom he loved. What an amazing comfort it must have been for him to think about the revelation of heaven, as he wrote, "There will be no more sea" (21:1). This reference is about separation. When a loved one dies, we feel the shock of separation. In addition, God's family is scattered all over the earth, separated by language, miles, customs and denomination. In that day, all separations will be eliminated. It will be homecoming and reunion for us all.

All tears will also be wiped away by our Lord in the comfort of the heaven of heavens! There will be no cause for weeping. Death will be gone forever. No more funerals! Cemeteries will not be needed. Pain and sickness will cease. Man will suffer no more in that land of health and happiness.

Sin will have no place in God's heaven. The curse is lifted there, and darkness is over. Everything is in the light of His shining face. Nothing will be done shamefully or secretly. All will be open and free. There will be no moral sins to drag the soul down. Crime, drunkenness, murder, lying, poverty, drug addictions and fighting will be gone forever!

Assurance of All Things New

There will be a new dwelling place in heaven. The city will be New Jerusalem. It will come out of heaven to a new earth. All believers will enjoy heaven. There we will walk its streets in new bodies not subject to disease, decay or death. We will bear a new name, because we have become new creatures in Jesus Christ.

The Answer to All Things Unknown

Especially in times of grief, Christians pose questions regarding what awaits us in heaven. Let us address a few of these questions.

1. Will we know each other in heaven? The answer is yes! Take comfort in these scriptures: 1 Corinthians 13:13; Matthew 8:11; Luke 16:19-31.

2. Will there be marriage in heaven? No. All physical relationships will change, even though our loves on this earth will continue (see Mark 12:18-25).

3. Will there be degrees of reward in heaven? Yes, the Bible speaks of crowns (see Revelation 3:11).

4. What will we do in heaven? We will have the joy and honor of serving our Lord Jesus (see Revelation 22:3).

5. Will there be little children in heaven? If children die before they are old enough to make a moral choice, they go to heaven. I do not believe they remain children. I believe that their spirit lives with the Lord and with the angels as tutors. In the Resurrection, they will be perfect and mature. I believe every child who has suffered will have a high place in glory. Heaven will be filled with children—mature and grown.

There remain many unanswered questions, but it is enough to know that Jesus does all things well.

Conclusion

Who will go to this glad place, the heaven of heavens? Only the saved will go in. If you are lost, your feet will never tread the streets of gold. Your eyes will never see the gladness and glory of that place. I want to go to heaven. I want to see the saints of all the ages. I want to hear the anthem of the saved. I want to see Jesus, most of all.

14
The End of the World Is Not the End of the World

In these days of war, a hysteria seems to grow concerning a possible end of the world. Popular movies in the past decade have adapted the theme of disaster and world-ending scenarios. In one, a giant meteor is on a crash course with Earth; in another, nations turn their nuclear weapons upon one another in a massive holocaust. The more dramatic the fear, the better the box office turnout!

I believe the movie industry simply echoes and feeds off the fears of our day. Besides the insanity in the Middle East, with crazed leaders trying to acquire biological and nuclear weapons, we also face a rash of new fears concerning natural disasters. Global warming, solar flares, changing weather patterns—all these prompt anxious debate. What does God's Word have to say about an end of the world?

This second epistle, beloved, I now write unto you; in both which I stir up your pure minds by way of remembrance: That ye may be mindful of the words which were spoken before by the holy prophets, and of the commandment of us the apostles of the Lord and Saviour: Knowing this first, that there shall come in the last days scoffers, walking after their own lusts, and saying, Where is the promise of his coming? for since the fathers fell asleep, all things continue as they were from the beginning of the creation. For this they willingly are ignorant of, that by the word of God the heavens were of old, and the earth standing out of the water and in the water: whereby the world that then was, being overflowed with water, perished: but the heavens and the earth, which are now, by the same word are kept in store, reserved unto fire against the day of judgment and perdition of ungodly men. But, beloved, be not ignorant of this one thing, that one day is with the Lord as a thousand years, and a thousand years as one day. The Lord is not slack concerning his promise, as some men count slackness; but is longsuffering to us-ward, not willing that any should perish, but that all should come to repentance. But the day of the Lord will come as a thief in the night; in the which the heavens shall pass away with a great noise, and the elements shall melt with fervent heat, the earth also and the works that are therein shall be burned up. Seeing then that all these things shall be dissolved, what manner of persons ought ye to be in all holy conversation and godliness, looking for and hasting unto the coming of the day of God, wherein the heavens being on fire shall be dissolved, and the elements shall melt with fervent heat? Nevertheless we, according to his promise, look for new heavens and a new earth, wherein dwelleth right-eousness (2 Peter 3:1-13, KJV).

Certainly the Book of Revelation teaches that war, death, plague and disaster are coming. Nowhere, how-ever, does the Bible teach an utter end to the world! Passages that we translate "end of the world" are mis-understood. In Matthew 28:20, the "end of the world" is the Greek word *aion* or "age," not *kosmos*, which is translated "world." Certainly, ages will come and go, yet the world will not end. Certainly the world will change, but it will not end.

Some take the literal view of prophecy, believing that there are seven years of judgment followed by 1,000 years of peace, while others don't take the num-bers literally. Either way, the Bible teaches there will be a lasting peace on earth following the awful judg-ments described in Revelation.

Practically speaking, many have viewed death as "the end of their world." At the time of a tragedy or breakup, some have thought the loss of love is the end of the world. Suicide is yet another way others think they can end the world for themselves. But the truth is, the world will not end literally or for you personally. You cannot escape from eternal realities.

There are strong, Scriptural reasons why the world cannot end.

The Word of God Sustains

The world is literally held together by the Word of God. Prophetic words must be fulfilled as spoken. The *word* (in Greek, *logos*) is keeping the world from utter destruction as it awaits the wrath of God.

There are supporting scriptures for this. John 1:1-3 tells us that the world was spoken into existence, "In the beginning was the word, and the word was with God, and the word was God without Him nothing was made that was made"

Hebrews 11:3 says that the worlds were *framed* by the Word (*rhema*) of God. God Almighty spoke the worlds into being.

Psalm 33:6 says, "By the word of the Lord were the heavens made and all the host of them by the breath of His mouth."

Some would point to the illustration of Noah and the subsequent warning of fiery destruction. Yet, did the world end at the Flood? No! Will the world end by fire? No! It will be renewed and made fit for inhabitants.

The Word of God always leaves hope for renewal! Colossians 1:15-19 tells us that Jesus Christ is the creator and the reason for the creation. Revelation 4:11 also reveals that the world was created for God's pleasure, and therefore will never end except at His good pleasure.

Our Hearts Tell Us the World Will Last

"God has set eternity in our hearts," states Ecclesiastes 3:11. There is something in every man that calls him to live! We do not want to die. Our destiny is more than a six- foot hole in the ground. There is the call of immortality in the soul of every man. Echoing in our literature is a cry to live. All of the efforts of thinking humanity lean toward living and leaving a legacy through work or monuments.

It is the cry of every individual to have eternal significance. Along the Appian Way in ancient Rome, researchers unearthed a tombstone. It said, "Here lies Titus Tollus; all who pass by say, 'Hail Titus Tollus.'"

Joseph Addison (1672-1719) wrote the play, *Cato*, in which the title character, Marcus Portius Cato, a Roman philosopher who lived before Christ, believed in a higher life beyond the myths of Rome. Cato says:

It must be so—Plato, thou reason'st well!—
Else whence this pleasing hope, this fond desire,

This longing after immortality?
Of whence this secret dread, and inward horror,
Of falling into naught? why shrinks, the soul
Back on herself and startles at destruction?
'Tis the divinity that stirs within us;
'Tis heaven itself, that points out an hereafter,
And intimates eternity to man.

—Act 5, Scene 1

We long for immortality! Wesley DuCharme wrote a book titled *Becoming Immortal*. It is not about salvation by grace, but salvation by technology. He states that nanotechnology will create tiny machines and computers that measure one-billionth of a meter, small enough to repair and replace human cells! The book's marketers advertised the volume this way: "If you've ever dreamed of seeing the future, expanding your life to the fullest, and living without fear of old age and disease . . . get this book!"

Man is driven to want to live forever. Age, pain and illness make us surrender. Yet God has provided a way to the future, to fullness, and to living without fear in Jesus Christ.

Heaven and Hell Stand Witness That the World Will Not End

In 2 Peter 3:9-13, we find described an "end of the age" scenario. Christ is coming in cataclysmic judgment on the earth. Fires of renewal shall change the earth into a new environment. This is exactly what happens to our bodies. I get a new body, but my personal world never ended. I will still be me! "We shall not all sleep, but we shall all be changed" (see 1 Corinthians 15:50-58).

There are other dimensions in which we shall live. John 14 promises the believer a wonderful life after death in heaven. We will also be heirs of a new earth!

In addition, Revelation 20 and 21 teach us that everyone will live forever. Your life will change, but will never end. You will either live with God or be separated from God forever. You cannot end your personal world through suicide. You will awake to find yourself standing before a holy God.

You cannot escape the responsibility to live and to experience life based on your choices. In the scriptures presented through this book, we have seen heaven and hell. We saw a terrifying scene before the throne of God, with the end for the lost being a lake of fire. We see a new city, a new heaven, a new earth, a new body, a new song, and a new environment for those who believe in Jesus.

Worlds don't end, they change! Life doesn't end, it changes. For whom will you live in the present? Where will you live in the hereafter?

This author sums it up:

I'm Going Home

Let others seek a home below,
Which flames devour, or waves o'erflow;
Be mine a happier lot to own,
A heav'nly mansion near the throne!

Then fail this earth, let stars decline,
And sun and moon refuse to shine;
All nature sing and cease to be,
That heav'nly mansion stands for me.

—William Hunter (1811-1877)